Reason to
Believe

Reason to Believe

Christian Faith for the 1990s

PETER MULLEN

SINCLAIR-STEVENSON

The author and publishers are grateful to Faber & Faber Ltd.
for permission to reproduce material by T. S. Eliot as follows:
lines from *Choruses from 'The Rock'* in the epigraph;
lines from *The Waste Land* on page 18.

First published in Great Britain in 1995
by Sinclair-Stevenson
an imprint of Reed Consumer Books Ltd
Michelin House, 81 Fulham Road, London SW3 6RB
and Auckland, Melbourne, Singapore and Toronto

A CIP catalogue record for this book
is available at the British Library
ISBN 1 85619 537 6

Typeset by ROM-Data Corporation Limited, Falmouth, Cornwall
Printed and bound in Great Britain
by Clays Ltd. St Ives plc

A little philosophy inclineth man's mind to atheism,
but depth in philosophy bringeth men's minds about
to religion.

I had rather believe all the fables in the legend,
and the Talmud, and the Alcoran, than that this
universal frame is without a mind.

Of Atheism, Francis Bacon (1561–1626)

Do you need to be told that whatever has been, can still be?
Do you need to be told that even such modest attainments
As you can boast in the way of polite society
Will hardly survive the Faith to which they owe their
significance?

Choruses from 'The Rock', T. S. Eliot (1888–1965)

Contents

Preface   ix

1   Why Does God Allow Suffering?   1

2   Is Anyone Listening? – Prayer   15

3   Living with Sin   41

4   Believing the Incarnation   59

5   The Truth of the Resurrection   73

6   The Femininity of God and Man   88

7   What Should We Teach the Children?   113

8   A National Church?   131

Preface

The word has got about that religion is out of date, that God has been superseded by modern science. It is not as if anyone has suddenly disproved the existence of God or marshalled evidence to show that the claims of faith are bogus; there is simply a climate of unbelief, a nebulous and ill-expressed opinion that talk about God is irrelevant.

The modern world is in love with its technological innovations and intoxicated by its efficiency and power. As far back as fifty years ago the influential German theologian Rudolf Bultmann wrote, 'It is impossible to believe in miracles in an age of electric light and the wireless.'

This is nonsense and, of course, such belief is not at all impossible. The intelligent arguments for God's existence, for the Incarnation and Resurrection of Jesus Christ, remain and it is not the case that they have been refuted, rather that they are so rarely stated.

The Churches themselves have accommodated themselves to modernity and, whereas once they might have claimed to be guided by the Spirit of God, they

seem nowadays to be driven only by the spirit of the age
– a mere whiff of the Zeitgeist.

As Bishop of Durham, the Rt. Revd David Jenkins
famously (or notoriously) denied the Virgin Birth and
the bodily Resurrection of Christ. But he is not the first
to do this. For the last thirty years – since Bishop John
Robinson's bestselling sceptical paperback *Honest To
God* – the drip, drip, of denial and debunking of traditional faith has issued from the religious publishers. The
spirit of the age, the bustling, technologically obsessed
attitude – mere fashion – has seemed to render the
traditional God and all his works as surplus to our
contemporary requirements and out of keeping with
our 'scientific enlightenment'.

This book restates the arguments for the traditional
Christian faith. It is a scandal that these arguments,
never refuted, continue to be subject to widespread
ignorance and misrepresentation.

You can be an intelligent, thoroughly modern person
and believe in God and believe that God has acted and
continues to act in the world. In fact this book concludes
that this belief, this standpoint, is the most reasonable
and persuasive of all the intelligent options now open
to us in the contemporary supermarket of ideas.

There are also practical and moral consequences.
With the loss of faith in God and the miracle stories of
the Bible, there has been a rejection of the idea of sin and
the need for redemption. The modern idea of technological mastery and no need of God also involves the
idea of 'progress'.

This idea of moral progress, that we are getting better
all the time, that we are not like our 'primitive' ances-
tors, is only a superstition. Is the age of Auschwitz and
Hiroshima, of napalm and the bomb – the age of James

Bulger's murder – less wicked, and so less in need of redemption, than earlier times?

This book re-examines the notion of evil and human wickedness and argues that we stand, as we always stood, in need of redemption and renewal.

It shows also that we must confront the fact that we all realise something has gone wrong in our national life. The social cohesion of earlier decades has been lost and there is widespread alarm at society's increasingly violent and lawless tendencies.

With this awareness there is a yearning for reconciliation and everywhere the longing for peace. There is talk of various citizens' charters and of the need to return to fundamentals. In all this is the plea for what might be termed 'a decent going-on'.

In fact this nation has had its share of troubles and social divisiveness in earlier ages. Out of these we evolved our policy for a decent going-on and it was known as The National Church, as the idea of Establishment.

This idea needs to be represented for our own time. It is one of the fundamentals to which we should return.

I have mentioned fundamentals, but I have no wish to compete with so-called 'fundamentalists' and this is not a stridently evangelical book; and it is not meant to coerce the reader. There is much that believer and non-believer have in common and this is bound to be so because we share a Christian cultural history. The answers to many of our psychological and social problems are found in this culture which is nothing less than the accumulated history and thought, art and science of the Western world over more than two thousand years.

Mainly because of our sophisticated technology and our instant communications system worldwide, we have come to be obsessed with what is new and enslaved by fashion and there is a prejudice against the past. But, as T. S. Eliot said, 'A people without history is not redeemed from time.' If we choose to ignore the past and refuse to interpret it to cast light on the present, then we are condemned to make all the mistakes of the past over and over again.

The answers to our contemporary malaise are to be discovered in our cultural inheritance. To keep on despising as 'not relevant' and out of date everything that happened before a week last Wednesday is a sort of willed insanity. We behave as if we believe that our contemporary pundits and columnists, sixpenny revivalists and the advertising men are to be heard rather than 'primitives' such as Aristotle and St Thomas Aquinas: because we have instant food, we imagine we can have instant wisdom too.

Besides, if our civilisation and culture has somehow been in the wrong all these centuries, on the basis of *what* is it now proposed to put it right? All iconoclastic and revolutionary proposals based on the mere ignorance of what has gone before are bound to fail.

Now, especially now, in an age when we have perfected the storage and retrieval of information, we have wonderful access to the whole history and thought of our civilisation. The fact is that this civilisation has been Christian and it is impossible to escape that particular influence: our common speech is alive with its echoes and all around us, in art and architecture, music and the attempts to frame public morality, the Christian legacy is palpable.

Let us put our Christian tradition to work, then, for our mutual society, help and comfort.

Peter Mullen
York, 1994

1

Why Does God Allow Suffering?

I should like to start with some words that are very personal, because the problem of suffering is not best expressed by abstract argument but by real human pain.

Very soon after I was ordained, I was asked by my vicar to take a funeral. When he told me the details, I wished myself a million miles away. I wished I had stayed in my nice safe career in the Civil Service and not got myself mixed up with all this religious business.

The baby had died in its cot, aged three months.

I found I had nothing to say to the parents. And, twenty years later, I would still not know what to say in the face of a similar grief. What, after all, could anyone say? Words fail in the presence of such pain. When the actress Billie Whitelaw turned up at the theatre late one morning and apologised to the author of the play she was starring in, she gave the reason that her father had died. The author, Samuel Beckett, said

nothing, but he covered his face with his fingers and
kept silence for a space.

Now, the point is this: even if, in such cases, you had
the most perfect and truest explanation it would still be
useless. For an explanation cannot give them what they
want; their father alive again, their child. In the face of
grief, explanations are gratuitous insults. They fail to
take account of the *depth* of suffering and bewilderment
that is being felt. It is as if, when the woman I love asks
me why I love her, I were to give her a diagrammatical
sketch of the workings of my internal body-chemistry.
And this is a true comparison, for moments of joy and
the tragic moment have this in common: they are beyond words. So you hold hands. You sit and weep with
them. Explanations are useless. You show your solidarity with them by sharing their grief and their
inarticulateness in the face of unbearable pain. That is,
literally, the meaning of 'compassion': feeling with.
Strangely, almost unbelievably, it usually works. And
it works because the event, the tragic death, is full of
energy. Death, like birth, is one of the great and inex-
haustible experiences we can have. Jung called it 'an
archetype' – that is, one of the mysterious experiences
which have set the pattern of all our experience from the
very beginning. The death, the intense grief, the expressed human sympathy, the theatrical trappings of
the funeral and the funeral tea – these help the bereaved
to cope, but they explain nothing.

So why, we may recollect in tranquillity, does God
allow suffering? Atheists and sceptics are in no doubt:
there is no God. David Hume argued on these lines:
Believers say that God is all-powerful and wholly good.
Whence, then, suffering? If suffering occurs because
God cannot do anything to prevent it, then he is not

all-powerful and therefore not God. If he can do something to prevent it, but does not, then he is not fit to be worshipped. The implied conclusion is, of course, that there is no God.

There are many subtle shifts employed by atheists and believers alike around this argument. For example, it is sometimes said that God allows certain evils in order that greater good may come. Wars are not only carnage and ruin, but they are also opportunities for the display of courage and love, devotion to duty and acts above and beyond the call of duty. Or perhaps the reason why parents are allowed to produce a subnormal or deformed child is so that they might grow and develop in love, understanding and self-sacrifice and thus become better human beings? Maybe temptation – which is evil – is permitted because the practice of resistance to temptation builds moral fibre, and nurtures true holiness?

But the sceptic argues that a God who depends upon evil to bring about good results is not all-powerful, and he is certainly less than morally perfect. This argument is strengthened by a further suggestion: even if we could accept a little evil so that there might be a whole collection of good results following, we surely cannot accept all the evil there is in the world? A God who requires so much evil in order that good may result is at best incompetent (i.e. not all-powerful) and at worst malevolent (i.e. certainly not good). In short, why is there *so much* evil? Surely, so the argument goes, even a God who is only fairly competent could have arranged a better world than this one?

Believers sometimes argue that evil has nothing to do with God at all. It is man's fault. God made the world perfect, but man, by his original disobedience, brought evil into God's good design. Suppose this is true, says the sceptic, it still points to a God who is less than all-powerful – therefore less than God. For being all-powerful includes having all knowledge. Why, then, knowing that evil would result – even if not directly by his own hand – did God choose to create the world rather than leave it uncreated? Why did God make the world when he could see beforehand that the result of his creative act would be suffering humanity? Once again, so it is argued, such a God is either impotent or malevolent or both, and therefore not worthy of our worship. He is only what William Blake called 'Nobodaddy' – nobody's daddy.

I should like to suggest a different solution to the so-called Problem of Evil. Suffering and evil are *necessary* if we are to be what we are – fully human.

There is a story by H. G. Wells called *The Time Machine*. Far ahead in the future, it is alleged, exists a generation of people called 'Eloi' who live a life of perfect bliss, untroubled by war or personal strife. However, the hollowness of their existence is shown up to horrifying effect by two events: first, when the time traveller from our own age asks them if they have any books, they show him a wonderful library – one which turns to dust as soon as he touches the book-covers, because they have never been read; secondly, when a young girl, drowning, cries out for help, the blissful Eloi ignore her, preferring instead to carry on dangling their toes in the stream and munching their paradisaical fruits. It is a nice touch of irony that Wells calls these bland, indifferent and uneducated drones 'Eloi' – the old Hebrew word for angels or gods.

If we are to be as we are, fully human, we must possess the faculty of choice. And any choice must be a real choice – a choice between things that matter. The only such choices are moral choices: that is, choices between good and evil. So, if we are to be really human, grown-up, mature, then it is necessary that there should be the possibility of choosing evil.

Would you sacrifice that which makes you distinctively human – your capacity for making choices that really matter, moral choices – for the existence enjoyed by the Eloi? Perhaps such an existence is superficially tempting, but, given time for reflection, few people, I think, would throw away their capacity to make real decisions in favour of a world as mindlessly and soullessly cosy as a television commercial. It would certainly mean throwing away the best we have, the highest expressions of human compassion and creativity: *Hamlet* and *King Lear*, Sophocles and the Mozart operas, the poetry of love and war.

All the virtues, all the grand words, are, as it were, in spite of evil. Where would triumph be if there were nothing to triumph *over*? What would be the value of love in a world where there was no hatred? Or consider this: one of our highest graces is forgiveness; and forgiveness is impossible unless there is sin.

In short, it is possible that we could have been created otherwise – like the Eloi, for example. But, if we had been created like that, one conclusion necessarily follows; we should not have been created human in any sense or degree of what we mean by the word 'human'. How can anyone ask for evil not to exist, for there to be no pain, when it is the fact of these sufferings which makes human virtue, human grandeur, possible, recognisable? We are human beings, not dumb pigs prodded by sticks and complaining that it hurts. Our humanity is exactly defined by our ability to triumph over evil. Therefore, to wish away the existence of evil is to deny the essence of ourselves. In fact, this is a logical oddity: for, on the basis of *what*, other than ourselves as we are, can we deny ourselves?

Perhaps we may fool ourselves and think that we could be like the Eloi and yet not like them – that we could enjoy all that bliss and yet not be as bland and irresponsible as they are? This is impossible. The Eloi may be beautiful, but they are subhuman. Humanity is defined as that which answers life's challenge. And life's challenge is to the triumph of love and goodness over suffering and evil. Therefore, evil and suffering are necessary counterparts of all that we honour and strive for.

This world of suffering and the relief of suffering, of disaster and triumph, was not made by God for his own entertainment. At the beginning of the Book of Genesis it states that God made men in his own image. This means that how life is for man is something like the life of the Godhead. I do not believe that God looks down on all our lives alternately bored and fascinated like a rich man at the circus. I believe he is also part of the ethical struggle which we have to face. When we suffer, God suffers, and this is demonstrated in the story of the life and death of Jesus.

The doctrine that God is without body, parts or passions, that he is above and beyond all feeling and especially suffering, owes more to the abstract idealism of Plato's thought in which God is 'The Form of the Good' than to biblical insights and stories which tell us again and again that, when his children suffer, God suffers too. He is said to care for us 'like as a father pitieth his own children'. He is shepherd to the flock. He loves us. In the person of Jesus he suffers for us, with us. This is all utterly biblical. It is a constant theme of a God who cares, who is not above feeling.

Could it have been otherwise? To go right back to the real or metaphorical beginning of time, could God have so made things that there would be no suffering in his creation? The answer must be No, for at least two reasons. First, all that is valuable and praiseworthy is what it is because it is a triumph over evil, difficulty and pain. Secondly, if God could have made a world without pain, he would have so made it. This is not to set a limit on God's power, to play into the hands of sceptics like David Hume. God is limited, certainly. But only by his own nature. We cannot understand the origins of the existence of pain and evil, just as we cannot understand the mystery of the origin of the universe. But the Bible and Christian tradition tell us that there is something unavoidable about pain and evil; unavoidable for God too.

I suggest that our understanding of this mystery is best helped by correctly understanding the meaning of the word 'creation'. Anyone who has ever seriously tried to write or paint or play the piano will tell you that creative fruits are grown only out of pain and struggle. No French without tears. The artist – take Van Gogh or Beethoven as excellent examples – knows that his art will cost him not less than everything. But no true artist will give up his efforts on that account. There is nowhere else for him to go except into his creative work. That work is his reason for living. It *is* him.

And a creation, a work of art, is not a diagram or a mechanism; it is alive. It has the capacity to move us to adoration or disgust. This is what the artist lives for: the creation of new life. And this is exactly what the Bible says about God. In the business of creativity there are no guarantees. The artist may believe, feel he has a vision; the artistic task of creativity is to realise that vision in words, paint, music or whatever. The possibility of failure always looms. God, like the artist, is, so to speak, playing this same dangerous game. The artist – one thinks again of Van Gogh or Kleist or Schubert – may die in the attempt. So did God in the person of Jesus Christ. The idea of God as an invulnerable Superbeing is a lie invented by people who are afraid to go to bed with the landing-light off. It is a babyish idea, superstitious idolatry. Understandable, yes – but an idea we must grow out of.

The whole game, the whole universe, life, its meaning and everything is summed up in that one word 'creativity'. Here is the constant struggle to fashion something marvellous out of materials that are (to say the least) less than perfect; to create something new and full of life. There is no substitute for it. God does not run the Civil Service with its circularised unadventurousness and its safety-first memos; he moves in the avenues of poets and among the violent clashes of the painter's colours, in – well, let us have a particular example – the perplexing motivation that made Mozart write the incredibly daring and incomprehensible (except to Haydn) opening of the String Quartet in C major K.465 – 'The Dissonance'.

You cannot have consonance if you do not have dissonance; you cannot have the flag of truth except it be over a battlefield of lies. And if you desire to bring order out of chaos, then first there must be chaos.

These are the highest things we know. Nietzsche said that we invent art so that we do not die of the truth. He was wrong – or, at least, he did not go far enough. He should have said that when we create great art we create truth. In the beginning was the word. Mozart, Shakespeare, Goethe, Van Gogh and others of the truly great, what were they doing with their lives except participating by grace and agony in the perplexities of God? This is a God who is no mere machine – *Deus ex Machina* – and who does not manufacture mechanisms, but who is alive and who creates life, risks it, bears it warts and all and, in Jesus Christ, dies to it on a gibbet outside the walls of the safe city, run by the Roman Civil Service.

St Paul expressed all this: 'The whole creation groans in travail.' This is what life is like. It could not be any different. God himself, being alive, is part of the same battle, involved in it. But what of the promise of an end to the battle, of the creation of 'a new heaven and a new earth' in which God will 'wipe away all tears from our eyes'? Isn't this a metaphorical way of describing the triumph of love over death, of redemption over suffering, which happens all the time in the here and now? Creative tension is resolved with the completion of the art work. Of course, then the process begins all over again. As W. H. Auden said, 'All that matters is the *next* poem.'

In the same way, every act of courage, of self-sacrifice; every bit of human decency cheerfully expressed, is a triumph over evil. Evil comes back and the battle is renewed. But evil can never triumph. That is the message of the Gospel. It can seem to triumph by its very severity and by its constant recurrence, but every time evil raises itself – and no matter to what heights – goodness rises to meet and overcome it. If you want the best examples of human goodness, look to where there was the most evil – the death camps, for instance, or Calvary. 'Father forgive them, for they know not what they do.'

When we begin to see the existence of evil as
something which is necessary because without it the
whole shape of our moral being and our human nature
would be different, we are bound to look critically at
our cowardice in the face of pain and suffering. For if
triumph over evil, personal bravery in the face of pain,
is praiseworthy – a fact which no one could deny – then
failure and fear when confronted with evil is a sign of
weakness. I do not say this weakness is inexcusable.
Who does not have some trepidation as he walks
through the valley of the shadow? But at least we know
that standards are set, have been set and will continue
to be set. We think of all the heroic acts of self-sacrifice
and courage which we have read about since the days
of our childhood. Of martyrdom. Of men substituting
themselves for children in the queues for the ovens at
Dachau. Of Captain Oates stepping out into the blizzard
so that his friends might save their lives. Heroes in war
and in the care of the sick. Women who have worked
themselves to the bone for their families. Christ who
expressed the greatest love by laying down his life for
his friends. These are standards we often fall short of.
We know that they are standards nonetheless. And they
are achieved in the face of suffering and evil. This means
that evil plays its part in shaping our moral nature, the
sorts of people we are. It is not good. Of course it is not
good, it is evil. But without evil there could be no good.
Moral opposition exists necessarily by contrast. Choice
is the supreme mark of human dignity. And that choice,
in order to be significant, has to be between matters of
the highest significance. This is the moral, human
struggle. The ground rules were set down a long time
ago:

'See, I have set before thee this day
life and good, death and evil. . . .'

(*Deuteronomy* 30:15)

Courage and perseverance, strength and unselfish-
ness in the face of pain and evil, is the greatest human
achievement. But this does not mean we should despise
others or ourselves when we give in and seem to be
overcome by our sufferings. This only produces guilt
and self-hatred in us – that is, even more evil. It was well
said that the Devil's first aim is to get us to despise
ourselves. Guilt is moral paralysis. Just because we
are not perfect does not mean we should give up the
struggle.

But it does no harm to look closely at some of our
motivations. Since the beginning of so-called 'modern'
times we have made a god of the Utilitarian philosophy.
And this philosophy states that the greatest good is the
avoidance of pain and the maximising of pleasure. It is
there in all the philosophers from Jeremy Bentham and
John Stuart Mill to the present day. It is politically
enshrined in the United States Constitution, which
speaks of 'Life, liberty and the pursuit of happiness'.

I can think of no better way to avoid happiness than
the pursuit of it. Real joy is accidental. C. S. Lewis wrote
about this under the title of his spiritual autobiography:
Surprised By Joy.

But this maximising of pleasure and minimising of
pain, what is it except what Nietzsche said of it – 'Pig
philosophy'? In present-day parlance we have a new
word for it: 'consumerism'. Human beings are frequently described as 'consumers'. What an insult this
is. What a perversion of our moral grandeur as beings
with significant choices. What – are all our choices

now only between one brand and its competitor? Consumerism is the modern technological version of the Utilitarian Pig philosophy which says that the most important thing in the world is the receipt of pleasure and the avoidance of pain. Of course, it is the most *pleasant* thing, but is it the most important thing, the most human thing? Are we really turned into what Thomas Carlyle said we would become – 'Patent digesters and Mayfair clothes-horses'? Is that all there is to life in the end – a perpetual search for the softest (and cheapest) option? Package holidays and pre-packaged food. A pill to wake you up, and a pill to send you to sleep. And, in between, an obsessive daily, glossy literature in newsprint and magazine devoted to the minutiae of diet and hairdo.

Suffering is bad. But there are worse things. The denial of our humanity is a much worse thing. The willingness to run grunting into the sty. The willing – even proud – acceptance of the epithet 'consumer'. Actually, we all agree on what is praiseworthy and honourable: every school child learns with awe of acts of heroism and the fate of the martyrs; no one assumes that a more glorious tale is to be told by the individual who has the exquisite acuteness of taste to be able to tell butter from margarine or one brand of chocolate-bar from another.

And yet all our newspaper and television channels define us as consumers, escapers of pain and pursuers of pleasure. This is a caricature of our moral stature, of our dignity as human beings. The exact thing that undermines our freedom and dignity, and all those fine-sounding words, is a thing such as that declaration in the American Constitution which already defines us as sub-human. To the sty, grunting.

And so we approach the thing that is truly evil: it is that which pretends there is no evil. That we have a right to be vacuously, empty-headedly and full-belliedly pleasured. That any discomfort is evil. It is not. The worst evil is the lie, that which misrepresents us. We are not – though we may in all our reading of the mass media be often tempted to be – Mayfair clotheshorses and Patent digesters. We are members of Christ, children of God and inheritors of the Kingdom of Heaven. No heaven without Good Friday. No French without tears. No triumph over pain without the experience of pain. No resurrection without a death.

When we say that evil is necessary, inevitable, this is not a counsel of despair. It is to say that God is in it too – because all that is the greatest and the highest, the most beautiful and the most tender, exists in constant opposition to evil. Good exists not as another option, rather than evil. Good only exists *in spite* of evil.

There is the mystery. That is the heart of it. When we tell the story of Good Friday and Easter, we acknowledge that God is involved in this mystery too. God is no manipulater of puppets, a knock-down argument for David Hume. He is at the centre of what is most serious.

And we are in it; all of us.
We do not know the outcome.
But we hope. We believe. Credo in unum Deum.

The most we can say, unless we choose to try to surpass or subvert St Paul, is:

'The whole creation groaneth and travaileth in pain together until now. And not only they, but ourselves also, which have the firstfruits of the spirit; even we ourselves groan within ourselves, waiting for the adoption, to wit, the redemption of our body.'

(*Romans* 8: 22–23)

2

Is Anyone Listening?
– Prayer

There is a joke among psychiatrists and psychologi-cally-minded priests which says: 'If you talk to God, that's prayer; if God talks to you, it's schizophrenia.' Every good joke hits a particular nail on the head – that is why we find them funny. And this nail is a particularly cruel and vexatious one: Does God answer prayer?

There is a whole spectrum of glibness covering this issue. I remember being much encouraged when I first heard the gospel for the fifth Sunday after Easter: 'Ask and ye shall receive'. So I asked. We won't go into what I asked for just now. Enough, perhaps, to say I was sixteen at the time. Anyhow, I did not receive it. I complained to the vicar, and he said, 'Ah, you must remember, when you pray, that God sometimes says Yes, sometimes says No, and sometimes says Wait.' Rather irreverently, if not illogically, I said under my breath, 'And what's the difference between saying those things and saying nothing at all?'

I remain unrepentant. That old vicar's cliché was a cop-out. If 'Ask and ye shall receive' means anything, it must mean that there are some things which, if you ask for them, you will get.

Of course, as we all do, I made – however imperfectly – the transition from childish (not to be confused with childlike) to grown-up religion. It was a circuitous route, via a congregation I joined in my twenties who used to pray for parking places for themselves in the town centre. Then I met another clergyman, and he told me that prayer has four parts to it: Adoration, Confession, Thanksgiving and Supplication.

Adoration

How do you go about adoring God? It can seem insincere, willing yourself to think and say things you do not feel. Worse, it can sound fey, wan and dreamy-eyed – reminiscent of black and white movies from the 1940s: 'Darling, I adore you!' There has first to be an awakening sense of beauty and awe – fear, even.

In my own experience, this took many forms, and I shall describe them not because I think that this must be how it is with everyone – it is not – but because, after years of talking to friends and parishioners about their experiences, there seems to be a lot of common ground.

Natural beauty stirs many people to a sense of awe. It may be a sunset over the sea or Wordsworth's 'host of golden daffodils'. With me it was – still is – mountains, their massiveness, the way they change colour according to the weather and the light; their outline against the sky. Orthodox spirituality teaches that we should not worship nature, but we may worship God through nature. We must not adore creation, but the Creator.

This is no doubt very sound theology, but in practice the line is a very fine one. What many people feel when they are awed (or overawed) by a natural scene is a sense that the landscape is haunted. There is a presence, a spirit. It is fashionable to mock primitive religious experience, imagining in our sophistication that it is not something primeval, but only for 'primitives'. But that primitive sense of not being alone in the world, or even that the world itself is somehow alive, personified, is not dismissed by being labelled 'Animism'. The sense of nature possessed by spirit is surely what Moses felt when he saw the burning-bush, the bush that burned and yet was not consumed. 'Take off thy shoes from off thy feet, for the ground whereon thou standest is holy ground.' The burning-bush was very likely not a super-natural event. Botanists, experts in the area, inform us that there is such a bush which glows as if on fire. Not supernatural, then, but the supernatural conveyed by what is spectacularly natural. And the response is awe, dread, adoration and holy fear.

Another man alone in a desert landscape, Jacob, awoke out of his dream of the ladder and exclaimed: 'How dreadful is this place! This is none other but the house of God, and this is the gate of heaven' (*Genesis* 28:17). And the prophet Daniel speaks of God as 'great and dreadful' (*Daniel* 9:4). It may be that in our own day, as we concentrate on the social meaning of the word 'God' as that which brings gentleness and togetherness – 'sharing', as one of the vogue words has it – we forget that he is holy and terrible and that this holy terror is often mediated by nature. We need to rekindle the awed and overawed sense. It is no accident that, in its secular image, 'dreadful' has lost all awesome connotations and may now be applied to a pork pie or a bad apple.

Poets refresh our language. Eliot restores to us the concept of dread in his words:

'Come in under the shadow of this red rock,
And I will show you something different from either
Your shadow at morning striding behind you
Or your shadow at evening rising to meet you;
I will show you fear in a handful of dust.'

It is an experience of holiness which goes back to Moses and Jacob. It belongs to the desert. Significantly, Eliot's poem in which those words appear is called *The Waste Land*.

Adoration, in its non-Hollywood sense, belongs to the world of what is religious, stark, taboo, holy. That is the original meaning of 'holy' – 'other' or 'different'. So it is not easy for us to recover our sense of what is holy or other in a society which is secular, where all phenomena are 'same'. The modern secular society is different from ancient (so-called 'primitive') societies in this respect: it is one-worldly and the sense of the 'other', the idea of the holy, has vanished. All phenomena come the same to science. But secular society cannot entirely expunge its religious past, and occasionally what is truly dreadful will break in upon our utilitarian dreams and frighten us. The experience is so debased these days that it is most likely to derive from a horror video.

Just as competence at the piano needs practice, just as moral improvement needs practice, so the cultivation of a sense of the holy needs practice. Our emotions need to be schooled, too. Nature is a place to look. Not so many years ago, I would have said that liturgy is a place to look as well. My own earliest experiences of church were of lights and colours, of soaring organ-music and of words that were worth their weight in glory. It is still possible to find these things, of course, but more difficult among the guitars and glee of modern liturgies. There is much to be said for liturgies which create a sense of togetherness and 'sharing', but it is a pity that these things are at the cost of our sense of what is other, awe-inspiring – adorable. Remove the sense of transcendence, and you destroy half of religion. We pay the price for trying to have a God who is fully house-trained.

This is a good time to say of adoration what should be said of all prayer: it is not for God's benefit, but for ours. God does not need anything of us. He certainly does not need to be adored. Rather, it is we who require to exercise the adoring, fearing and reverencing faculty if we are to be fully human. There is something in us which needs to worship. This applies to believers and atheists alike, to churchgoers and non-churchgoers. For it is, after all, from the psychological point of view, nothing other than the appreciation of the mystery of the world, its vast beauty and strangeness and – as a consequence – the smallness and fragility of every individual 'I'. You do not need to be a churchgoer to be able to say these words:

'I will consider thy heavens, even the works of
                                                  thy fingers:
The moon and the stars which thou hast ordained.
What is man, that thou art mindful of him?
And the son of man, that thou visitest him?'

                                                  (*Psalm* 8: 3–4)

It is not even necessary that there should be a God who made the heavens. Anyone who goes out on a starlit night and feels nothing as he gazes into the vault of the sky has not much humanity in him – to say nothing of the religious sense.

> 'Look at the stars! Look, look up at the skies!
> O look at all the fire-folk sitting in the air!
> The bright boroughs, the circle-citadels, there!'
> (*The Starlight Night*, G. M. Hopkins)

A sense of adoring and wonder is necessary to being human because it is the one thing that gives us a sense of perspective regarding ourselves and our place in the universe. For if we do not perceive ourselves rightly, we shall not have a context in which we can act rightly. This, in the broadest sense, is what is meant by saying that morality derives from religion.

Confession

The second in the quartet of praying attitudes is confession and I shall write about this in the chapter on sin. Once again, it is not God who requires our confessions. The point is that we confess for our own benefit, to increase our awareness of our faults so that we can begin to do something about them. There is one sense in which confession is for God's benefit, however, and that is if we think of God not just in his transcendence but in his indwelling aspect. St Irenaeus taught that, for all the ravages of Original Sin, the Image of God (Imago Dei) is not extinguished within us. It lives in us as a potential perfection, a wholeness of the personality. Obviously, then, owning up to our sins and beginning to overcome them goes some way to mitigate the effects of Original Sin and to build up the wholesome Image of God within us. Even the atheist can say that the self-awareness that goes with genuine sorrow for our faults tones down our habitual beastliness and makes us more determined to do better.

Thanksgiving

Thanksgiving is the third prayerful attitude. Its psychological value consists in the sense of well-being and the reduction of anxiety which it brings. 'Count your blessings' is a cliché because it is true. Even the poorest person has something to be thankful for. Paradoxically, it is usually the poorest who are the most cheerful in giving thanks. The insensitive, bored, cynical rich man, rushing from one surfeit of pleasures to the next in his posh car is an image well-grounded in fact. Whatever the characteristic sins of the poor, boredom and cynicism do not feature prominently among them.

I used to visit an old man, a parishioner, who was crippled with arthritis. He sat in his window all day and watched the weather. He never had a bad word for the weather whatever it was doing. And his wife said he had always been the same, even in his days as a farmer when he had had to go out in it daily.

This man, Bill, had what I would describe as a thankful nature. He was simply grateful for the privilege of being alive. He once expressed this to me: 'My joints are so bad, I'm grateful to be able to unscrew the tops of my bottles of brown ale.'

This was not mere flippancy. He meant it. He had cultivated the habit of thankfulness.

Is it all right to give thanks for material benefits? The Jews of the Old Testament thought so. This was because they – like the medieval Christians – had a sense of the oneness of creation which was, for them, neither soulless matter nor disembodied spirit, but spirit incarnate in matter. It has always been a heresy to prize spiritual things over material things *just because they are spiritual*. Even if these two categories could be separated, it would still be true that there are good spiritual things and bad spiritual things. 'Try the spirits whether they are of God.' (*I John* 4:1)

And another good result of thanksgiving is that it should encourage our generosity. When, by giving thanks, we draw our own attention to how much we have got, we might be stirred to give some of it away.

Thanksgiving, like all prayer, builds up our sense of perspective, puts us in our place. When you give thanks, what are you giving thanks *for*? Well, we give thanks for what we value. And what we value tells us what we ourselves are worth. Ask yourself what you are most thankful for and see what that tells you about yourself. Confession is individual and, in a good and necessary sense, ego-centred. *I* am responsible for *my* sins. Thanksgiving is the opposite faculty, psychologically speaking, for it concentrates the mind on what I am not responsible for, on what is given to me. It teaches me that there exist things and qualities in the world that do not originate with me, are not my fault and are not created out of any virtue I might possess.

There is the special sense of thanksgiving which belongs to the Holy Communion, the Eucharist – εύχαριστω is the Greek New Testament word, meaning 'I give thanks'. In this service the Christian gives thanks for his redemption through the body and blood of

Christ. This is what the act of Communion is for: the reminding of the Christian to whom he owes his redemption. 'Do this in remembrance of me'. Once again the old Greek word illuminates the truth: ἀνάμνησις, 'calling to mind' – literally, 'against amnesia' or, as we say in Remembrance Day services, 'Lest we forget'. Every Holy Communion is a Service lest we forget. Not because, if we did not do it, Christ would feel unappreciated, but because, by calling to mind the mode of our redemption, we are doing something which makes the experience of redemption real in the present.

The Eucharistic thanksgiving is more than a word of thanks. It is a sacrament. Instead of saying something, at the central point of the service, the worshipper does something: he takes the bread and wine of Communion. To an unbeliever, this is a meaningless act, a gratuitous act; but for the believer it is a sacramental act and full of meaning. Gratuitous acts and sacramental acts have something in common: they require a context in order for them to be understood. The taking of the bread and wine for the Christian is a sacramental act because it belongs in the context of the faith, of belief – which is precisely why it is meaningless or gratuitous to the unbeliever who does not share that context of faith.

At the climax of the Eucharist, words of thanksgiving run out and, in silence, the communicant performs the central act of thanksgiving and anamnesis: he takes the bread and wine. This is entirely right, for, whenever the core of faith's mystery is approached, all words fail and something must be *done*, almost as it were gratuitously. The water is poured in Baptism. The ring is given and received in Matrimony. Earth is scattered over the coffin at the Burial of the Dead. All these gestures are responses to the central mystery which can be approached by means of words, but which cannot be encompassed by words. In all cases, they are a sort of thanksgiving because they are a heartfelt acceptance of what *is*: redemption by Christ's death; two people made one flesh by their promises; a member initiated and accepted into the tradition; another committed to the mercy of God.

Acts of thanksgiving happen in secular life too. To make a gift of flowers, to offer a kiss, a handshake; to prepare a meal for guests – all these are secular sacraments in the sense that their full meaning can only be understood when the context in which they arise is understood. What makes them Sacramental (or sacramental) acts of thanksgiving is the participant's tacit acceptance of the context to which they belong; and that acceptance is symbolised and represented by the act itself. Actions, as another cliché says, speak louder than words sometimes.

Supplication

The fourth attitude of prayer is supplication or intercession. It is perhaps the most difficult of them all. Everyone has asked at some time or other that a sick person might be healed. In the chapter on pain and suffering I have tried to say something about why God does not always heal the sick. So what is the use of praying for the sick? It might seem that – even if there is a God who can make sick people well again – God acts as he pleases irrespective of whether we pray or not. Indeed, it would be a strange God who healed only those who are well-prayed-for. What about the lonely sufferer who has none to pray for him? This sort of selective healing does not say much for God's much vaunted compassion. And it works both ways – a double-bind – for God often seems not to heal those who are most prayed-for either. In fact, to a detached observer, there no doubt seems a great deal of arbitrariness about the whole affair.

In that chapter on suffering, I have tried to say how God does not observe our pain but enters into it. So here I will confine myself to saying something about how God's entering into our pain looks from *our* point of view – from the perspective of the supplicator.

First, in a small way, our act of praying for the sick or the distressed person is like God's infinitely larger act of entering that person's pain. It shows our care. We may not actually feel his pain, but there is something in sincere sympathy (feeling-with) that is very much like it.

Secondly, our prayerful sympathy may extend as far as practical help and comfort.

Thirdly, those who are sick are often helped and cheered by the knowledge that they are being prayed for.

Finally, the act of supplication is an act of solidarity – first of all between man and God, who cares for us; and so between persons also. We are all in the same boat. *All* flesh is grass. 'Ask not for whom the bell tolls; it tolls for thee.'

Rituals, Meditation & Contemplation

This has been only a sketch of four sorts of prayer, four approaches to it. They are ways-in, if you like, whose religious and psychological value I have tried to describe. Of course, there are other ways – thousands of them – and books abound on the subject. At one end of the scheme there are those manuals which prescribe a very strict routine of mental prayer and physical labour – such as *The Spiritual Exercises* of St Ignatius Loyola, the founder of the Jesuits. At the other end, there are teachings which advise us not to worry too much about the formal aspects of prayer, but simply to offer oneself every moment to God. Many people have found Pierre de Caussade's book *Self Abandonment to Divine Providence* valuable.

Actually, the Ignatian and the Caussadian methods are only explicit religious schemes to fit two of the most prominent dispositions known to us all: there is the man who is never happy unless he has his whole day's programme mapped out before him, and he belongs to Ignatius Loyola's school whether he knows it or not; then there is the man who is prepared to meet everything as he comes to it, and this is the psychological disposition which belongs to Caussade's way. Most of us are somewhere in between, happiest with a measure of spontaneity to unfasten the desirably secure routine.

I should like to talk about prayer in the broadest sense – prayer as it may be understood and practised by believer and unbeliever alike. At bottom, prayer is a response to God through our experience of him, or else in the unbeliever's terms it may be seen as simply a response to our experience. From our point of view – that of our individual subjectivity – it does not matter whether we take and use the believer's language and image or the unbeliever's. The psychology of human response is the same in either case. This must be so since we all inhabit the same planet, live roughly the same lifespan and are preoccupied with the same basic needs and desires: for food, drink, sex, sleep and the need for love and a way of making sense of the world. This is why we can all – except fanatics – talk to one another usefully. And it is worth remembering that there are secular fanatics as well as religious ones. Sometimes it appears that the National Secular Society and the Governors of Iran have very little between them when it comes to the Principle of Intolerance.

Our prayers and rituals are clustered about our desires and preoccupations. It is because sexual love is so powerful that it is connected with at least three sacramental rites: Baptism, Confirmation (the Christianised form of ancient rites which acknowledge a young person's coming to fertility) and Matrimony. Every religion has rites to cover these archetypal events. Secularism, rejecting religious rites, forms its own – the main example of which is the Register Office marriage, of course.

Food and drink feature in the rituals of all the world's faiths. And they have been formalised in secular society in a hundred ways, from the Sunday Lunch to the Cocktail Lounge, from Chocolates on Mother's Day to the Office Christmas Party – none of which have more than a tenuous connection with accepted religious forms, except, of course, they have become pseudo-religious forms of their own. Perhaps I am even underrating the power of ritual as inescapable in human life when I say 'pseudo'? Some of these new observances have taken on all the authority of older rites: football is a religion with its gods, its demons, its drink and its songs as primitive as anything you can find east of Java. The legendary football manager Bill Shankly was asked whether he regarded football as a

matter of life and death and he famously replied, 'Oh
no, it's much more serious than that!' How about the
Management Induction Course as a bureaucratised version of ancient initiation rites? If the ancient fertility rites
would not have been complete without their tantric
dancing, where is our modern wedding without its
disco? In the ancient rite, the Medicine Man or the
Shaman was supposed to remember and recall, at subsequent meetings, all that had taken place: nowadays
we have the video instead. The psychology is the same;
only the technology has changed.

Our thoughts follow our desires and necessities. This
is why every man will form words to express his grief
and longing, his ecstasy and his quest for meaning.
Anyone, religious or secular, with an ounce of sensitiv-
ity will boggle after a minute's reflection on the vast,
glorious and awful cosmos and his own place in it. This
boggling is the beginning of prayer. This searching for
love, for rest, for joy and understanding, is the beginning of prayer. It is what St Paul calls 'groaning'. The
whole universe groans in travail.

This searching and groaning has for thousands of
years been expressed in the art of civilisations. In the
artwork, the artist confronts the central mystery and
tries, somehow, to respond to it by depicting it – so that
he can say to his neighbour, 'Look, life's like this, isn't
it?' Because we are one species on one planet, it follows
that we can talk to Sophocles and Samuel Beckett, to the
Aztecs and Mozart. Our attention to artworks is a form
of prayer because it is an attempt to visualise, hear,
understand and respond to the wonder of all created
things. It follows that the things of our own civilisation
will mean more to us than more distant perceptions and
creations. That is the very definition of a language and

a cultural tradition. It is practice that makes perfect, and that, incidentally, is the main reason for applying ourselves purposefully to our Western tradition in art: so many men and women chewing over the same problems in similar words and visions for centuries: a degree of fluency must surely be accepted to have resulted – even by the most nihilistic. (Actually, our contemporaneously 'most nihilistic' – Samuel Beckett – is also the most fluent!)

In pursuing an art, man apes God: he tries to create something out of nothing. On the human scale, he faces the same danger which God faced when he began creation – danger of love and death, freedom and pain – the danger that all could come to dust. So art, because it is concerned with these things, is part of the life of prayer.

Work, ordinary routine work, is also a kind of prayer. The discipline of routine application is commendable. The workman apes God as surely as the artist: the exercise in both cases is that of bringing order out of chaos. And, if God's act of creation was an example of omnipotence limiting itself – simply by choosing to make *this* rather than *that* – then routine work is a similar act of self-limitation on our part by which we will ourselves to persevere at a course of action decided upon. Work is prayer. The monks knew it: *Laborare est Orare.*

Art and work – Kunst and Arbeit, as the two doors of the Temple of Wisdom are called in *The Magic Flute* – are forms of prayer, of bringing order out of chaos – whether it be in a poem and 'the intolerable struggle with words and meanings', or else with a patch of weeds. In prayer (art, work) we join with the Word (the λογος) in the perpetual task of giving form to what is formless (a mere groan) and to making rational what is inchoate. Prayer is not just 'a form of words' and the echo of a holy thump onto the kneeler in the pew. It is the realisation of the world – knowing it, understanding what and how it is – through reflection and longing for truth and knowledge. You might say one of man's earliest prayers was the act of naming the creatures in the Garden of Eden.

These sorts of prayers, though not 'forms of words', are wordy and physical: bringing order out of chaos, poetry out of babel and a rose garden out of a pile of ash. But there are other forms of prayer, and perhaps these are even more important.

There is the work of charity. Put like that, it sounds like an example of religiosity of the stuffiest sort, enough to dissuade anyone from prayer for ever. Nuns in grey gowns with greyer faces. Monks full of misery and mortification. 'Cold as charity' – you can see where the expression is derived from. But it is not like that. Charity – the Greek word is ἀγαπη, love – is a burning fire. Charity is a work and an art at the same time. It means having the imagination and warm-heartedness to feel what your neighbour is feeling and to act for him as you would for yourself under exactly the same circumstances as he finds himself in. It is prayer because all prayer is offering, sacrifice: and it will cost you something. It is prayer because it is the chosen reversal of the normal scheme of things. It is the work and art of behaving towards the other person as if he were yourself. As Kierkegaard said, 'We are all subjective towards ourselves and objective towards others. The true task is to become objective towards ourselves and subjective towards others.'

That is, we must rejoice in others' joys and weep in

others' woes. What is the point in what seems like this obliteration of my own personality? It brings to mind all those Hollywood movies about sickeningly sanctimonious nuns who kill people by doing hypocritical good to them; who do good not because, by prayer, they have learned to so desire – but because it is commanded of them: hair shirts and an absence of humour. No one responds better to a command than a masochist. Trouble is, a masochist will never help anyone – least of all himself – for his masochism is only the introverted form of his sadism.

In charity our own personality is not obliterated. What *is* destroyed is self-obsession and self-pity, which is the most destructive thing there is. When my concern is the concerns of others, I am set free from my own concerns. I must confess that I am not very good at it, but I will admit this: whenever I have tried, even half-heartedly and with mixed motives, to give someone a helping hand, I have myself received an unexpected leg-up. Now, if that sort of thing can happen when we have mixed motives, what trans-formation of our lives would take place if we could *really* exercise charity?

'Teach our faint desires to rise,
And bring all heaven before our eyes!'

The most appalling thing about the Christian faith is that it is psychologically true, and thus inescapable. You can doubt God and you can curse Christ. You can say that the Bible story is a grotesque and 'primitive' fiction. You can scream that the Church is a rich man's conspir-acy to keep the poor in their place. And yet, when you have done all that, you come up against:

'The thing I would not, that I do. . . .'
'Who art wont to give us more than either we
                         desire or deserve. . . .'
'Neither do I condemn thee. . . .'
'Who of thy tender mercy didst give thine only
                                    Son. . . .'
'Our Father. . . .'
'. . . forgive them, for they know not what they do.'

And, like the disciples on the road to Emmaus, our
hearts burn within us. For, as soon as we try to practise
the prayerful way of charity, we know it to be the right
way, and that every other way limits us more and more:
limits us in the most severe way possible – by making
us the victims of our own desires. There are horrible
negativities: some religious people's attitude to the
things of their religion is like the alcoholic's attitude
towards drink – no joy in it any longer, but a grim
obsession, a masochistic sense of obligation and a derogatory vehemence to all who will not join the same
party. But charity, as we know, covers a multitude of
sins. Translate that how you will: there's nothing better
than sympathy for an antidote to falling short. We all
fall short. So we all need charity. There is no such thing
as a dispenser of charity.

One of the highest forms of prayer has always been
thought to be that which is called Contemplation: not
saying or thinking anything at all, but the silencing of
words and thoughts before the central mystery –
whether you would want to call that mystery 'God',
'The meaning of the World' or just 'experience'. At the
end of a book which tried to lay bare the mystery of
understanding, Wittgenstein said, 'What we cannot
speak about, we must commit to silence' (*Tractatus*

Logico Philosophicus). When we consider, with the Psalmist, the moon and the stars, we know that all we merely *say* about them – or about the cliffs and the tides, the birds and the lizards, that have been here for millions of years before we arrived, and which will supersede us by as many million millennia, no doubt – is as nothing compared with the universe itself. It is the universe which gives us our context. We can offer it nothing that it needs. So God's answer to the querulous Job:

> 'Where wast thou when I laid the foundations of the earth? Declare, if thou hast understanding. . . . Whereupon are the foundations thereof fastened? or who laid the corner-stone thereof; when the morning stars sang together and all the sons of God shouted for joy. . . .
>
> 'Canst thou bind the sweet influences of Pleiades, or loose the bands of Orion? Canst thou bring forth Mazzaroth in his season? Or canst thou guide Arcturus?'

No? Well, better shut up then. And that is the aim and method of contemplative prayer – to keep mental silence, to banish thinking, the internal dialogue and the endless jabber which makes me think that I, and not Orion and the Pleiades, am the most important thing in the universe.

Since the 1960s days of 'Flower Power', muesli and Hinduism by Numbers, there has been a lot of what I can only call nonreligious interest in religious things. Spiritual 'states of consciousness' have been 'evaluated' and the results of contemplation and meditation have been quantified in terms of 'reduction of adrenalin', increase of 'Alpha brain waves' and 'rapid eye movements'. It is all rather tedious, this scientific study of spirituality – there is even a 'laboratory of human spirituality' in Oxford, which for sheer incongruity resembles the attempt to practise embroidery with pogo sticks. But at least it shows that even the modern scientific worldview has had to come to terms with the practical results of spiritual practices.

It is – for what it is worth – true that people who take up regular prayer in the form of meditation and contemplation feel better, look fresher, drink less and generally become less anxiety-ridden than those who do not pray. We have known this for thousands of years, of course, just as we have known that there are no hard-and-fast rules about what exactly constitutes prayer. Is the old man regularly bent over his pint and his dominoes engaged in a form of contemplative activity, or is he wasting his time in the grip of a useless habit? Ask him. Is the shepherd out walking the hills merely doing an arduous job, albeit in the fresh air, or is he involved, even if only half-consciously, in an act of spiritual pilgrimage and personal development? Read some of the medieval classics on the subject – for example *Piers Ploughman*.

There is a great deal of evidence to say that, while effort and imagination in prayer – particularly in meditation, visualising biblical scenes and putting oneself into them as a participant or a bystander – brings rewards, the highest form of prayer is a sort of willed detachment, an emptying of the mind: a silence. This is contemplation.

If intercessory prayer apes God's compassionate entering into our pain and suffering, then contemplation copies God's self-emptying (as described in the second chapter of St Paul's epistle to the *Philippians*) in order to become man in the flesh. It is a further confirmation of that incarnational insight that the world is one – spirit and matter – and that God and man are indestructibly linked. Our task is his task. Our psychology is not different in kind from God's very being, but only in degree. This is what St Ignatius said when he wrote that the Image of God within us is not obliterated by Original Sin.

It is also close to the mystical doctrine that he who prays and he who answers prayer are one. But then mystics have always tended towards monism – the doctrine of the essential oneness of Creator and creation – and for this they have often been condemned as heretics. Perhaps such fine distinctions between what is Orthodox and what is Heretical should be left to the Inquisition – the spiritual equivalent of the accountants? It remains to say we should be impoverished without the 'heretical' insights of such monists as Gregory of Nyassa, Benedict Spinoza and, in some of his rarest moments, St Paul himself.

Contemplation is the nearest thing in this life to freedom from the constraints of time and space. Decently accomplished – I say 'decently' because it is never perfectly achieved except by the greatest saints – it is like death itself, or eternal life. It is deliberate, wakeful, non-drugged extinction of ordinary consciousness: literally, a going into silence. The jabbering ego is quieted. Nothing, consciously, is going on at all.

Those who become great masters of this form of prayer – 'masters', but there are more women than men – usually develop a knowledgeable spiritual silence in their ordinary, everyday lives as well. It is as if they are regular travellers in a strange land about which the rest of us know nothing – or else we fumble over maps and diagrams of a terrain which these masters have walked.

Contemplation is a mental condition into which the saints embarked daily, nightly. It is a sort of creative way of doing nothing. I speak banally, but then I am trying only to describe its psychological appearances and not the spiritual truth which it actually *is*. How could I do that? How could anyone – since that willed venture into the darkness and the silence is the best and highest of all we know? In everyday life you may spot a contemplative by his disinterestedness. It may look like boredom. You may think he is dreaming, miles away, or merely rude. No. I think he has gone into a state which allows his unconsciousness to work within the context of time. *Something* is going on. It is not restricted by logical reasoning – at least not conscious logical reasoning – but the result, when the contemplative returns to the ordinary world of discourse, is always characterised by its sublime expression of reason, its *form*. Mozart was like this. Fretful, nervous at a dinner-party, unable to be *in* the chatter he himself emitted. Nowhere, really. Well, not consciously. It turned out in his music often just where he had been.

Those who only practise these perfections, who are not spiritual geniuses, know the value of silence. The inward silence that can exist while the contemplative is in a tube station or a traffic jam. It is like nothing else in human endeavour. It is a taste of death brought into life which – in the interim – makes life more lively. It is a bit of the next world in this world. It may even be 'the next stage in our evolution' or some such thing as the laboratory for evaluating religious response would love it to be.

The results of contemplation are a growth in reticence and charity. The silence decentres the contemplative, makes him less concerned with himself, makes him perceive himself from another centre – perhaps from something like God's point of view. It induces that Kierkegaardian sense of objectivity towards oneself and subjectivity towards others.

Contemplation, once begun, seems to absorb the contemplative like an extra duty – though it is a duty which makes all his other duties easier to fulfil. I believe it to be the prayer to which Our Lord returned daily. It is the ladder of perfection, what St John of the Cross called *The Ascent of Mount Carmel*.

There is a caution: of all the gifts coveted by human beings, spiritual gifts come highest; and to desire spiritual gifts as a will to power is to court disaster. Spiritual growth is not for one's own benefit but for an increase in charity. The craving for spiritual power so that one will be admired or desired by others is the road to darkness and witchcraft. It is the way of self-destruction. Religion and prayer is all paradoxes. If you seek to enhance yourself, you will destroy yourself. If you lose yourself in spiritual exercises for their own sake, you will find yourself.

> 'He that findeth his life shall lose it:
> and he that loseth his life for my sake
> shall find it.'

> (*Matthew* 10:39)

There is a story about a monk who, having first begun contemplative prayer, received visions. He ran to the Father Abbot:

'Father, I've received a vision of St John!'

'What were you doing at the time?'

'Why, praying, of course!' said the young monk avidly.

The next morning: 'Now, Father, I've seen Our Lady in a vision!'

'Were you praying at the time?'

(Even more avidly) 'Oh *yes*, Father!'

And the third time: 'Last night Our Lord himself appeared to me!'

'Well, son,' the old abbot replied, 'we must do something about these visions – they seem to be taking your mind off your prayers.'

The aim is not self-aggrandisement, magic and spectacular tricks, but an increase in reticence and charity.

Should you try it? It must be said that contemplative prayer is not like the latest diet or health fad. There are signs that you ought to begin. The main sign is chronic boredom with the world at large, with religion and prayers in particular. Anxiety, fretfulness, loss of patience, the oppression of tediousness – in short, a sort of spiritual nausea. Only silence can cure this.

It should not be attempted for more than ten minutes at first. It is very difficult. You will find that you can still the mind for a few seconds, and then all the babel of words and images – the reckless flight of ideas – will come rushing back. Do not be discouraged. It is not a *performance* you are looking for, as in weight-lifting. The trying is what counts. You may find, in time, that you wish or need to practise this form of prayer for longer periods. You may also find it loathsome yet need to continue. It is the hardest thing there is. It is exhausting and yet, in the paradoxical way of religious experience, it is exhilarating and it gives energy. The only sure test that this is the right sort of prayer for you is an increase of charity in your everyday life: but you will be the last person to notice that!

As the years go by, you will spend more and more time in contemplation, and it will be tiring. But it will have become a necessity. It will be to you what composition was to Mozart: 'I work because it fatigues me less than anything else.'

If visions and insights come, all well and good. But remember the young monk! Visions are not the goal. It is all about the increase in charity, becoming more Godlike. There will be dryness and boredom, anguish and an almost constant sense of failure and unworthiness, the feeling that you are a hypocrite. You will get depressed and even nihilistic, certainly doubting God and suspecting there is no point to your prayers. You may even experience what John of the Cross calls 'the dark night'. None of this matters. If you get as far as that, you will continue with regular contemplation to the end of your life.

Contemplation will absorb the four parts of prayer into itself. This will seem to happen in a formless way, but really there is a form which is all under the surface of consciousness and which, consequently, can only be revealed in retrospect. That is not important, either. You will occasionally feel an enormous sense of God's wonder. Or you may feel the weight of your own sins as truly intolerable. You will have moments of the most overawed and tenderest thankfulness. A person may come into your prayers in the form of a name or an image. You will learn to act on these promptings.

There is little more to be said, for, if you get as far as that, you will have no need for books on prayer.

One thing more about the theology of it all: it works. It is true whether you use the 'God language' to describe it, or whether you use a different vocabulary altogether – Depth Psychology, for example. That does not matter. The theology or psychology is to the act of contemplation only what the beads are to the Prayer of the Rosary. A word may be said in favour of talking about prayer in the 'God language' simply because that language has been used for so long that it has grown into a traditional repository of wisdom. Might as well avail ourselves of it, then. It saves a lot of spadework. Use an atheistic vocabulary if you wish, but it will mean an awful lot of translating has got to be done if you are to communicate with those in the past who have trodden the same path. You can talk about contemplation in terms of God or the Absurd. The experience is the same.

I return to the quotation at the beginning of this chapter: 'Ask and you shall receive.' What, then, may we ask for if not parking places in the town centre or to become a millionaire? We may ask for an increase in charity, or in any of the virtues. If we ask for these things, we shall receive them. The reason is clear enough: if we get so far as to ask for them, it means we already desire them. If you keep asking God to make you less bad-tempered, more patient, kinder, then you are on your way to becoming like that.

Virtue, like anything else, takes practice. Augustine tells us we have to become hypocrites – actors who put on a mask – and act *as if* we are virtuous until we *become* virtuous.

Prayer of whatever kind is a work. It may, from time to time, be joyful, sorrowful or plain tedious.

It is always an act of the will.

3

Living with Sin

Sin means sex to the tabloid newspapers. And 'living in sin' – a doctrine basic to Genesis and St Paul – means living an adulterous life. Really, sin includes a lot more than that: pride, vainglory, envy, hatred, malice, back-biting and all uncharitableness, for example. But when was the last time a Cabinet Minister was forced to resign because of his uncharitableness? Or who was the last member of the Mothers' Union to be expelled for back-biting? We are very selective in our disapproval. We are also hypocritical. The tabloids love a steamy story, so I suppose that must mean a great number of us love a steamy story too – because the tabloids sell in their millions. But, while we applaud a cheerful adulterer – especially if he is a Cabinet Minister or a 'Television Personality' – we sometimes join in the calls for his resignation on the grounds of morality.

This is the caricature, comic-strip picture of sin. When it comes to discussing sin as a reality which infects the whole of our lives – so that, in a much deeper

Reason to Believe

sense, we really are 'living in sin' – then we become most offended. If you were seriously to accuse someone of being a sinner these days – as St Paul accused the whole of mankind in his day – you would be regarded as an impolite, ill-mannered person. To call someone a sinner is almost as bad as calling him a bad driver ... or a poor lover. We think we have outgrown sin. Our language gives us away. We talk of being 'emancipated', 'liberated' and 'enlightened', 'liberal'. The idea that our moral nature may in fact be contaminated seems to us repugnant and unworthy. There is even something archaic and biblical – smelling of dusty Sunday School rooms and the Methodist Hymnbook – about the very issue of morality. We are modern people with videos and microwave ovens. We do not want our technologically slick lives to be sullied over by the notion of ethical fallibility. Live and let live.

The idea of sin really went out when women were enfranchised, capital punishment was abolished and homosexual acts between consenting adults in private became universally tolerated if not approved. There was a psychological revolution: 'Thou Shalt Not' was replaced by 'All You Need Is Love'. Well, Augustine said something similar: 'Love God, and do what you will'. The 1960s simply left off the first two words of that injunction. Everything morality had formerly spoken of as a matter of public concern and, even, obligation became only a matter of 'personal lifestyle', of what anyone in particular might be 'into'. You 'did your own thing'. Sin, as a notion governing personal morality, was associated with blimpish characters like retired colonels in Kent and Mrs Mary Whitehouse.

Curiously, at the same time, the sense of corporate sin increased. Everyone, in these last twenty years, has

become more guilty about nuclear weapons, mass starvation, global warming and the hole in the ozone layer.
It seems to me a strange thing that culpability of the
many should be substituted for culpability of the individual. For sin is the consequence of the exercise of
choice. And it is individuals who choose. Moreover, to
claim that individuals are enlightened, emancipated
and okay while society – which is made up of individuals – is irresponsible and inconsiderate to the point of
self-destruction seems to be a contradiction in terms.
Sinful, in fact. Odd that I should be held responsible for
the ozone layer, but not for sleeping with my
neighbour's wife.

Sin, as a concept or a doctrine, is unfashionable because any idea of authority – of someone telling you
what is right and what is wrong – is unfashionable. But
what if certain things *are*, as a matter of fact, wrong?
Surely we ought to be warned about these things, put
wise as it were to the tripwires? How could we go about
demonstrating that something is wrong, some deed or
practice sinful? From the point of view of the individual, we might start with the Ten Commandments.

There is, to begin with, some confusion about what a
commandment is. I have heard liberal-minded teachers
of religion say things like, 'Some people regard these
commandments as binding.' This is misleading, a misunderstanding of the nature of a commandment. It is
not a suggestion or a political compromise, a bit of
utilitarian give-and-take: a commandment is a *commandment*. It is something you are not asked to do, but
told. 'Thou shalt not steal' does not mean 'Wouldn't it
be jolly nice if we all agreed not to steal?' It means 'Don't
steal!' The response to a commandment is to obey it.
Otherwise, there are penalties. The Ten Command-

ments, then, are exactly what they say they are: they are not the Ten Suggestions.

Moreover, they are part of a relationship – what the Old Testament calls a 'covenant' – between God and his people. God, through the mouths of his prophets, repeatedly tells his people that, if they will obey his Commandments, all will go well with them; but, if they disobey, things will go badly. Some people insist on looking at this covenant in a narrow way, as if to accuse God of being irritable, moody, a spoilsport and angry if things do not go his way. This is a misunderstanding of the spirituality, the psychology, of the Commandments. They are not issued for God's benefit, but for the benefit of his people. This is to say that they are the bare ethical bones of a whole community's life. They are what is *morally necessary*. This is why they are commandments, and not mere suggestions. They *must* be obeyed because, when they are disobeyed, life goes awry.

Let me leave theft, sex and murder on one side for a minute and concentrate on the commandment 'Honour thy father and thy mother'. Why should we do this? Why is it morally necessary to obey it? Well, because 'honour' means 'respect', 'listen to', 'pay attention to', 'learn from'. Honouring father and mother means giving intelligent attention to the experience of the past – in short, to tradition. The infant knows nothing to begin with. He cannot even blow his nose until he is shown how. His parents' tradition shapes his life; indeed they give him all that he can call his life: manners, knowledge, understanding, language. Without those things, a growing person is less than a person. To grow to manhood without them makes him less than a man.

The Book of Exodus expresses it exactly: 'Honour thy father and thy mother that thy days may be long in the land which the Lord thy God giveth thee.' It does not mean 'If you don't look after Mum and Dad, you'll die young', it means 'If you want to live an intelligent life, based on sound experience and good reason – if you want to avoid the worst mistakes – then pay attention to the tradition in which you are raised'. Again, the commandment is not for God's benefit, but for ours.

Indeed, there does not even need to be a God for these commandments to be morally necessary. They are the distillation of commonsense: commonsense so clear and distinct that it is what we call 'holy'. The Commandments are indubitably right. And this can be seen immediately by anyone foolish enough to proclaim their opposites. Just try saying:

'Steal!'

'Murder!'

'Commit adultery!'

'Covet everything that is your neighbour's!'

'Tell lies!'

'Take no notice of your parents!'

. . . and see what sort of society would result if these 'commandments' were obeyed. It would be no society at all, of course, only anarchy and chaos. This is an illustration of what is meant by saying that the Ten Commandments – God or no God – are morally necessary. Hell is the biblical punishment for those who break the moral law. Whatever doubts you may entertain about a hell beyond the grave after this life, there can be no doubt that the moral chaos which would follow wholesale disobedience to the Commandments would be a hell on earth. I say 'would be', but, as a matter of fact, we have experience of this chaos: murders, theft, vandalism and violence, broken homes, envy, hatred, malice and all uncharitableness.

So, when I talk about sin in this chapter, I mean nothing more nor less than a description of what happens when we deny that which is morally necessary.

Of course, despite what religious fundamentalists – or even some atheists – believe, the issue is not black and white. For the reality is not universal obedience; neither is it wholesale disobedience: it is a bit of both. As St Paul says, 'All have sinned and fallen short of the glory of God.' The word he uses for 'sin' is similar to the word he uses for 'falling short'. It is taken from the Greek games, from the archery contest. The 'sinful' arrows are those which fall short of the target. We all fall short of the moral necessity. Our obedience is always imperfect.

What can we do about this? The Bible, in both Testaments, is utterly clear: 'Repent'. Face up to what you have done wrong and admit it. Commonsense, again, really. Simply an acknowledgement of the moral necessity which, temporarily, you had abrogated. It is to say, 'Although I may not always live up to the perfection of the moral law, I know the moral law is true and eternal, universally binding, and that I endanger myself and others when I fall short of it – i.e. Sin.' To repent is to return to what you know to be true – know because it is indubitable; indubitable because to contradict it does not make sense, only contradiction and nonsense. There is a way in which moral rules are grammatical rules: they belong to the very meaning and consistency of what we say. And repentance is not an act of grovelling demanded by the irate God; it is a reasonable return to what we know to be true, inescapable.

As soon as we begin to give any thought to these matters, the question arises as to why, if the moral law is so plainly sensible and universally beneficial, we ever depart from it. One of the answers traditionally given is that we do so because of Original Sin – because our hearts incline to evil, that is to say because we are perverse: in acting according to what we think are our best interests, we actually act against them. If we steal or enter an illicit sexual relationship, we may think we are doing ourselves good, adding to the sum total of our private pleasurable experiences. It may feel like this, but this is not the truth. And it is no use claiming that I might get away with it, even if I offend and endanger society, my neighbour, by the rules which hold us all together. I may seem for a time to get away with it, but what thief does not live in terror of being caught, or what adulterer escapes family and personal anguish, rows, bitterness, acrimony or the distress of children?

Watching detective stories on television is a national pastime. Our family divides between Ruth Rendell and Inspector Morse. It was Dostoevsky in *Crime and Punishment* who used a detective story to demonstrate excruciatingly that 'guilty' means more than just getting caught for what you have done wrong.

The young man Raskolnikov brutally murders an old woman. Even as he fends off the questions of the ace detective Porfiry, he is haunted and tortured by visions – flashbacks – of his crime. The feelings of remorse and worthlessness produced by these recollections hurt Raskolnikov far more than any externally administered punishments enacted by the law.

No one escapes these things. And the next thing to Original Sin – emotionally speaking – is Original Guilt. Again, contemporary thought and fashion teaches us that guilt is something unhealthy, and therefore to be avoided. It is not unhealthy if it leads us to the knowledge that we are in the wrong and encourages us to put things right. Sometimes this can be done, as it is done in personal relationships. People do, after all, apologise sometimes.

Unfortunately, it is not usually so simple. For the doctrine of Original Sin says that, while we have some measure of choice in moral matters, that choice is not unlimited. Our hearts are said to incline to evil. Sin begins thus to look not simply like a perverse act, here and there, but a stain on our character, a disease, a taint. Yes, and we are all tarred with the same brush. We do not want to sin, and yet we sin repeatedly. St Paul expressed the whole human/moral crisis perfectly: 'The thing I would not, that I do; and what I would, I do not.' Human psychology summed up in fifteen words of one syllable!

What can we do in this crisis?

We can renew our moral efforts, of course; but it is dispiriting to find oneself falling into the same pit time after time. Most of our sins are sins of habit, so that they seem almost to be traits of our character: a bad temper, idleness, furtive lust or whatever it may be. Our own moral efforts never satisfy us. The only man to be proud of his virtue is a hypocrite, whereas it is the saint who is most dissatisfied with his personal morality. The closer we are to original goodness, the more heavily do we feel the burden of Original Sin.

Fortunately, lonely moral striving is not the only route open to us. St Paul speaks about an antidote to sin which he calls 'grace'. Grace is not a magical means by which sin is flushed out of us, like detergent cleansing a blocked drain. It is what ensures that, though we are always hindered by our sins, we are not entirely bound by them. By grace, we are capable of goodness as well as evil, and it is the goodness which matters most.

In fact, we notice that good and evil are not entirely distinct, but related to each other in complex and – in this life, at any rate – indissoluble ways. I mean, our virtues are the mirror images of our vices. The very quality that makes a man earn a reputation for meanness is what drives him to a decent scrupulousness in business. Dismiss a man for what seems like a selfish preoccupation and you may find you have dismissed an expert, or even an artistic genius. In the war film *The Dirty Dozen* it was criminals whose violence and expert cunning – undesirable attributes in a peaceful society – were put to good use against the enemy.

It is well known among the prophets, and St Paul himself, that irritability and impatience go hand in hand with a zeal to see that right prevails and that the word of God is proclaimed. Grace does not make life all sweetness and light, but it does ensure that all experience is not bitter and black.

The paradoxes of morality are endless, including the paradox that too much introspection of our sinfulness can itself become sinful. The way to overcome to some measure our sinful aspects is to do something else instead. But what? Small acts of kindness and generosity. Application to a task in hand whatever it is. The monks knew that 'Work is Prayer'. Practise diligence. Practise an art or a science – for virtue and virtuosity are closely connected. A work well done, whether it is a room springcleaned, a vegetable patch dug or a new symphony in G minor, is itself a piece of goodness. So the bad-tempered man who keeps a beautiful garden is not utterly bound by his sins – look at his garden! Beethoven did more good in his music than evil by his irascibility. Ordinary human kindness can cover a multitude of sins, as the woman who washed Our Lord's feet and

dried them with her hair discovered. In the old language of spirituality, the Devil wants to hold us bound
in our sins, for that dismal condition multiplies evil.
Grace frees us from our sins even while we persist in
them. St Paul knew this too. But, when he asked himself
whether we should sin the more so that grace may more
abound, he answered, 'God forbid!'

Sins are there to be forgiven. And it is *people* who
forgive sins, so that forgiving one another's sins is the
very condition upon which we ourselves are forgiven.
'Forgive us our trespasses, as we forgive those who
trespass against us.' Jesus told Peter and the disciples:
'Whosoever's sins ye remit, they are remitted; and
whosoever's sins ye retain, they are retained.'

This is not to invest the disciples with a magical
power but simply to state the profound truth which is
at the centre of our lives together – that forgiving sins
gets rid of sins, while refusing forgiveness increases the
power and persistence of sin. We know from our own
experience that this is true, but it is, unfortunately, our
habit to deny our experience and to go on making the
same old mistakes. Let me illustrate the truth about
forgiveness by giving you a most banal and rustic example:

A few years ago at a Garden Party in our village,
someone took offence at what someone else had said to
them. It is human to give offence from time to time: we
all do it. And it is human to take offence. But it is also
rather better humanity to make up the quarrel and
forget the offence. As it happened, neither of these two
people would budge. They do not speak to each other
at public meetings and they avoid one another in the
street. That offence persists because it is unforgiven. In
Jesus' words, the sin is retained. It spoils part of the lives

of those two people, and, because the rest of the village knows about the attrition, it festers like a small wound in the whole community.

If one of those people would only go to the other and say 'Sorry!' the whole trouble would be over and done with. It would vanish immediately. The sin would be remitted. Pride prevents them. That is why pride is called 'The Chiefest of Sins' – because it prohibits forgiveness.

Our falling-short, our moral bad archery as it were, does need to be owned up to. This can be done in ordinary human relationships, but, for some, it needs to be done in a formal, ritual style and the words of forgiveness are required to be heard. This is why the church provides two Confessions in the Prayer Book.

These are sometimes criticised today by people who do not like language about sin at all, and who certainly have no time for statements like: 'We acknowledge and bewail our manifold sins and wickedness . . . the remembrance of them is grievous unto us, the burden of them is intolerable.' But any priest of experience, any psychiatrist, will tell you that the sad parishioner or patient bowed down and hamstrung by guilt feels exactly as the Prayer Book defines the sinner. The burden *is* intolerable. The remembrance of sins *is* grievous – that is, it actually hurts, that it all but puts a stop to the conduct of daily life. I have met people so disturbed by unhealed wrongs in their past that they dare not go out of the house, spend their time in gloom and idle misery. There are also those manically obsessed with sin and guilt, constantly washing and rewashing their hands, cleaning their homes until they shine like a sterilised laboratory, all in the attempt to cleanse themselves from the guilt of past offences.

What needs to be done if relief is to be found is a certain amount of acknowledging and bewailing. In case this doctrine should sound archaic and, in the fashionable phrase, 'irrelevant', let us be reminded that Sigmund Freud said the same thing. In order to get rid of repressed guilt which finds its outlet in neurosis and all kinds of obsessions and compulsions which mar our lives in the present, we must go back into the past and from there articulate the wrongs and hurts that cause our present suffering. The process is called psychoanalysis. You go back to your childhood and start from there. The gospel says the same: 'Ye must become as a little child.'

How can the reality of sin be denied by even the most fully paid-up demythologised modernist when we see all around us the results of sin and guilt unexpiated? Neuroses. Psychoses. Obsessions. Compulsions. People 'screwed-up', manic or depressed. If 'sin' means anything, this is what it means: what else but a crippling neurosis – a fear to go out of the house – represents a *falling-short* of the full life we are always hoping to live? The destructive reality of sin and guilt is all around us. Only, when it is expressed in the clichés of chapel pews and dusty hymnbooks it sounds unpersuasive. We know its existence is real and frightening enough, however, because we observe spoilt lives all around us; we feel in ourselves the crippling influence that the knowledge we have fallen short brings. So we need to talk it out: with God in the Prayer Book Confessions; with our neighbours with whom we have fallen short by falling out; with a priest, maybe, at Confession; or with a psychiatrist who knows about the destructive power of human guilt; with a friend who has a listening ear. The mode does not matter. There are many ways of

lightening the intolerable burden, of sharing the grievous remembrance. Yes, a grief shared is a grief halved.

The Prayer Book speaks of 'acknowledging and
bewailing', while Freudian psychology speaks of
'catharsis' (the old Greek word for cleansing). But it is
all one. The boil has to be lanced or the demon exor-
cised. There is no way to cope with sin and guilt other
than the way of expiation. 'Whosoever's sins ye remit,
they are remitted; and whosoever's sins ye retain, they
are retained.' All that prevents the expiation of sin is the
refusal to face up to it. No wonder that the modern
world, which has no time for the concept of sin, is as
neurotic as it is! Its illusory pride in its 'enlightenment'
hides its dissatisfaction with itself, its disease. The shal-
lowness of contemporary thought on the matter of sin
is revealed by contemporary events: does a century
which has given us two World Wars, the concentration
camps, Hiroshima, napalm, germ-warfare and mass-
starvation really have no room for the notion of sin?

Does current technological optimism and consumerism wish to deny that there has been some 'falling-
short'? How could it, in the light of events? We must
deal with the sin, the taint, the shortfall, somehow. It is
encouraging to me to discover that the methods by
which we cope have always an underlying psychological similarity. We cannot cope all alone: the ancient
Jew needed a scapegoat to drive off into the wilderness
bearing his sins; the Christian needs Christ the Redeemer; the perplexed modern needs his analyst with
whom he can establish 'transference' – that is, the com-
munication of basic psychological and moral states; we
all need sympathetic confidantes and friends who will
remit our sins, accept us, shortfall and all.

The word 'sin' may sound old-fashioned, but the

comparison with archery is illuminating. You can use many other expressions to describe the condition that 'sin' used to describe, but you cannot deny the fact of sin, of falling-short. 'Who is there without sin among you?' As the Prayer Book says, 'If we say we have no sin, we deceive ourselves and the truth is not in us.'

Surely it is obvious that the person who considers himself to be perfect is deluded? And the delusion is dangerous, like any lie is dangerous, for it misrepresents what *is*. Constantly falling short into sin, into bad habits and habitual weakness, is morally and psychologically debilitating even when we know we are doing these things. When we deny our sinfulness, we do deceive ourselves. We misperceive ourselves, and that can lead to severe disturbances of the personality – to psychosis and full-blown insanity in the extreme; to what an older tradition saw as so disruptive a force that it used such words as 'demonic possession'.

If we want to live a healthy life, we must see ourselves as we are and be a little more accepting of ourselves. 'Love your neighbour as yourself' means you must love yourself first. And self-love is not egocentricity or making excuses for ourselves. It is a sense of perspective on ourselves. 'Know thyself,' as Socrates said. That is where a life without delusions really begins.

For any sensitive person, a certain amount of self-loathing is unavoidable. But there should be a limit set on this. Too much wallowing only leads to more mud. Of course there should be striving for moral improvement – what would it mean to claim there should not be? But the end of all our striving is to see ourselves as we are. Moreover, the striving for improvement should not be so very deliberate or self-conscious, for that itself is a kind of self-indulgence.

It is rather a case of re-centring our aspirations and point of view. Instead of concentrating on *me* all the time – even me and my sins – I should do something which I know to be constructive: work; see what bits of kindness I might accomplish; apply myself to a study, an art or a craft; learn.

In terms of palpable evil, there is as much if not more stultifying negativity (the biblical word is 'damnation') in the man who concentrates all the time on his sins as there is in the unreflecting wicked-doer. Self-obsession (the biblical word is 'pride') is the worst thing there is, whatever form it takes. The antidotes are kindness, work and application to something else. I should like to take an example from music: Gustav Mahler (1860–1911) was one of the most obsessed, and even self-obsessed, people imaginable. But by turning the substance of his obsessiveness into a musical description of what human life is like – and into a prescription for some of its ills – he transcended his obsessiveness and gave the whole world for all time something that is of actual spiritual help: the symphonies. Much the same can be said of Mozart's obsessive creativity – why write three of the greatest symphonies ever when you know there is little prospect of their being performed? Then there is Van Gogh's depressive profusion in the painting of pictures.

Dirt must be turned into love. Grace says it can be. Personal discontent can be transformed into a work which does untold good. I think of poor, mad William Cowper who turned his obsession with his sinfulness, and the conviction that he was certain to be damned, into lines that have, no doubt, saved many people from despair these last two hundred years:

'Can a woman's tender care,
Cease toward the child she bear?
Yes, she may forgetful be,
Yet will I remember thee.'

No doubt Cowper's sense of sin went a long way to
provoking those words in him. But the words themselves
transcend the sense of sin and so become – because of
Cowper's application of disquieting emotion and a tortured intellect into poetry – a blessing to the rest of us.

Delius did the same.

And Wittgenstein. Once, when Wittgenstein was
pacing the floor in the early hours, Bertrand Russell
asked him, 'Are you thinking about logic or your sins?'

'Both,' replied Wittgenstein.

Well, his sins are of no account to us. But his work on
logic – created out of fear, guilt and panic – is a benefit
for us all.

Anyone who does something decent with the energy
that comes with his guilt does all of us a service. I do not
care that the gardener makes his show of perfect blooms
out of a sense of manic futility; I enjoy the garden. It is
a pity that Mahler was so often distressed . . . but then,
we have the symphonies.

Another of the paradoxes of morality is that there
seems to need to be some distress, some horror, loathing
and nothingness in order for something lovely to break
forth. As St Paul might have said, where sin is, grace
more abounds.

Formal, ritual confession to a priest is helpful to
many. It can seem to combine scapegoat, redeemer and
transferential psychiatrist and soulmate all in one. What
is interesting about this ritual is the idea of penance. I
remember going to Confession before my Confirmation

when I was seventeen. Actually I had had a rather restrictive Protestant upbringing and the suggestion that I should make confession to a priest brought flooding back all those lurid phrases about the Church of Rome as the Scarlet Woman and the Pope as Antichrist. I had been taught by hateful innuendo to despise the Confessional into which people walked 'reading the *News of the World*, insincerely confessed their sins, then walked out of a side door and opened the scandal sheet again'.

Because all the other Confirmation candidates had agreed to go, I agreed too – which might at least say something about the triumph of solidarity over prejudice. I confessed such desultory misdemeanours as I could recollect at the age of seventeen and I was most surprised to receive a penance which seemed to have nothing at all to do with my sins: it was to pray the Magnificat every day and to double the time taken over piano-practice.

It was my first instruction into the truth that the best thing to do about your sins once you have acknowledged and bewailed them is something completely different. I suppose I had expected to be asked to recriminate bloodily with myself, to turn myself inside out with anguish and remorse. What I was actually told was to go away and do something decent and useful instead. It has been the same every time I have visited the Confessional. May I suggest to non-Catholics that they forget the bloodcurdling slogans about the Scarlet Woman and Babylon the Great Harlot and get along to Confession if they are troubled by guilt. The priest, or the vicar or curate, generally has an inkling of exactly what needs to be done to relieve the sense of oppression and to provide constructive moral advice.

I mentioned solidarity and there is a solidarity among sinners. Honour among thieves. We have all sinned and fallen short of the glory of God. You can take comfort in that, even if it means that the Sinners Club is not very exclusive. Most of us fall for one of two errors: either we deny the fact of sin – which is simply to delude ourselves and so preclude on our own behalf any possibility of improvement in self-knowledge; or else we imagine our sins to be greater than they are, filthy rags, myself the Chiefest of Sinners – St Paul thought this of himself. The first error puts us in a fool's paradise of self-deception while the second is itself a sin, a colossal arrogance, a form of pride, an unproductive self-preoccupation.

Relieved of my guilt at that first Confession, I did not scratch around for a lost copy of *News of the World*, but I did come out of church feeling cheerfully lightheaded. Not because my sins had been scarlet and now they were white as snow, but precisely because the vicar had shown me that I was neither as bad as I feared I might be nor as good as I wanted to imagine myself.

That experience is the dawning of a sense of perspective, and the odd thing in the paradoxical world of the psychology of morals is that there is no sense of perspective without first a sense of where I stand as an individual. It was Clive James, in a piece of television criticism, who gloriously defined a sense of humour as 'a sense of perspective dancing'.

That is what makes of a sense of sin not an archaic euphemism for sexual misbehaviour but an absolute moral necessity.

4

Believing
the Incarnation

'The Word was made flesh and dwelt among us, and
we beheld his glory; the glory as of the only begotten of
the Father, full of grace and truth.'

That is the climax of the Gospel for Christmas Day
and it is one of the earliest summaries of official Christian doctrine's proclamation that Christ is God as well
as man. In every Holy Communion Service the Nicene
Creed is recited, and this is even more explicit and
definitive than the Christmas Gospel:

'. . . Lord Jesus Christ, the only begotten Son of God,
begotten of his Father before all worlds. God of God,
Light of Light, Very God of Very God, begotten, not
made, Being of one substance with the Father . . . who
for us men, and for our salvation, came down from
heaven and was incarnate by the Holy Ghost of the
Virgin Mary, and was made man.'

The Nicene Creed dates from AD 325 and so it is
one of the most ancient and venerable statements of
classic doctrine. It has been celebrated in the Latin

Mass and portrayed in Western art for more than a
thousand years. But the claim that Christ is divine,
that the man Jesus, as he strode about Galilee, par-
took of the divine nature, has always been
contentious. The Nicene Creed itself was written in
an attempt to settle a dispute which arose out of the
teachings of Arius who did not believe that Christ
was God. ἦν ποτε ὅτε οὐκ ἦν – sang Arius and his
disciples: 'There was a time when He was not.' In
other words, Jesus Christ is not one in Being with the
eternal God, maker of heaven and earth. (And Arius
really did sing his heresy. He and his supporters
formed something like a minstrel band or a pop
group and they sang in chorus 'There was a time
when he was not.')

It is easy to sympathise with Arius, and with all those
who have agreed with him down the centuries, from
Nicea to the authors of a book which first appeared in
the 1970s called *The Myth of God Incarnate*. For how can
a man be a God? It is crucial to notice that Christian
doctrine says Jesus Christ was truly man and truly God.
His manhood was not obliterated by his divinity –
contrary to what some well-known hymns mislead-
ingly suggest. As in Wesley's line, 'Veiled in flesh the
Godhead see . . .'

If Wesley had wanted more accurately to represent
the teaching of the Christmas Gospel, he would have
written not 'veiled' but '*Revealed* in flesh the Godhead
see'. 'Veiled' suggests Jesus was hiding his divinity,
whereas the Gospel speaks of his divine nature as revealed in his life.

Many people – even churchgoers – share Arius' scepticism about Christ's divine nature. They are ready to
admit that he was a good man – perhaps the best man

ever – but to claim that he was more than that – more than a saint and a great prophet – seems to many to be going too far.

There is the objection of particularity. How could *one* man only partake of the divine nature? This has even been called a scandal.

In our own times, objections to Christ's divinity are much more likely to arise out of the frankly anti-supernaturalistic world view. The idea of a supernatural world, a transcendent realm linking itself to the world of our solid flesh, seems an alien idea, vaguely embarrassing, archaic, out of sympathy with the spirit of the age which is this-worldly, materialistic.

I have tried to show in many other parts of this book that the materialistic assumption is only a prejudice, a fashionable presumption. I do not need to go over that whole argument again, but this is clear enough: once we accept that the materialist, this-worldly presumption is only a fashionable prejudice, then there is no longer any necessity to regard it as a reasonable criticism of super-naturalist arguments in general and the supernatural doctrine of the Incarnation in particular.

Difficulties in accepting the truth of the Incarnation start with earlier difficulties concerning the nature of God. It has been said that the creed of the Englishman is that 'There is no God, and it is wise to pray to him from time to time.'

And there is some truth in it. We are rightly reticent about proclaiming what the nature of God is. There is a sort of ordinary reverence which knows instinctively, unconsciously, that it does not do to say too much about God. This is for the very good reason, as we know, that, if there is a God, then his ways are indeed higher than our ways and his thoughts are higher than our thoughts.

Why make fools of ourselves, therefore, by trying to know too much about him?

That 'creed of the Englishman' might be amplified as follows:

> 'I believe in a Higher Power. Somebody, after all, must have made all the galaxies and things. I certainly believe in Jesus Christ who did a lot of good and said things that we all know to be true. He is a great example to all of us. If only we could be more like him, the world would be a far better place. It's a pity they crucified him. I'm a bit embarrassed by all this stuff about the Incarnation. I mean, that sort of thing just doesn't happen, does it? But I believe in Christmas. It's nice for the children to be told something about their religion. And there's a nice spirit – know what I mean? People are a bit nicer. . . .'

This is, of course, a parody, but I do not think it is too much of a parody of what people think about Christianity – the Incarnational aspect in particular – in England today. The Nicene Creed and the New Testament and Christian tradition of nearly two thousand years say something quite different. They say what St John, putting words into the mouth of Jesus, said: 'I [Jesus] and the Father are one.'

Even some of those who are not beguiled by the materialist prejudice and who might therefore accept the reality of a supernatural world often think that St John and Church doctrine go too far. How could anyone presume to know so much about the nature of God that he dares speculate, and even pronounce, on the relationship between God and the man Jesus? Such presumption seems so un-English. It may be all right for the Latin races with their processions and statues and

'Ave . . . Ave . . .' under the hot sun, but over here we are more reticent.

I should like to argue that the doctrine of the Incarnation is not an arrogant presumption, but a revelation of the truth. First, I should say that, while revelation can take the form of a sudden blinding flash – as in the case of St Paul on the road to Damascus – it does not usually happen like that. If something is revealed, it is indubitable, beyond doubt. And the way in which anything becomes indubitable is by long experience which constantly strengthens and reinforces an opinion, a way of believing or seeing, until other opinions – rivals for our credence – come to seem unconvincing.

I believe that the Incarnation says something which is undeniably true about the relationship between God and man, between divinity and humanity. In the broadest possible terms, it says that there is solidarity between the two. The Nicene Creed says this too, but it uses words from a philosophical vocabulary with which we are no longer familiar. It talks about 'substance' in a sense of that word derived from Aristotle and the Greeks. It is the same with its use of 'Person'. It uses the words 'Father' and 'Son' in a way that is out of step with our normal understanding of those words. But, if we translate those ancient usages into the terms of our contemporary understanding, what we arrive at is something like this:

'In the beginning was the Word. . . .'	'There is a rational principle governing the universe. . . .'
'. . . and the Word was with God, and the Word was God. . . .'	'This rational principle is part of God, but it is not the whole of what we mean by the word "God". . . .'

'In him was life, and the life was the light of men. . . .'	'This is where all life and intelligence originates and by which it is sustained. . . .'
'And the Word was made flesh and dwelt among us. . . .'	'That rational principle is manifest not only in the eternal world but in this world. It is the same principle, there and here. . . .'
'Full of grace and truth.'	'The rational principle – i.e. Word or λογος – is not an abstract idea but a person- ality. Whatever we mean by "person", God is at least a Person . . .'

To make contemporary sense of the Incarnation, we have to understand that the language of its classical expression is metaphorical: there is, for example, no way in which 'He came down from heaven' can be construed as literally true – for the very good and obvious reason that heaven is not 'up'.

In the New Testament, St John is the writer who has the most to say on the subject. He constantly character- ises the Incarnation as the manifestation of Life, Light, Truth and Love: those words sound in almost every verse of the Gospel and the Epistles. Life, Light, Truth and Love for St John belong to what he calls the Word – to the underlying principle of creative rationality in the world. It follows that death, darkness, lies and hatred are not part of creative rationality – the Word or λογος. The proclamation of the doctrine of the Incarna- tion is therefore Gospel, good news; for it says that what we need and value most in this world, in each individual lifetime, is eternally true.

A moment's practical reasoning supports this. Death has no reality, no characteristics. It is the mere absence of life from which we derive all characteristics. Darkness is only the absence of light. It is the very principle of generalisation – against all classification, naming and choosing: i.e. against the Word. Lies are a perversion of language. Language is used to say what is, and what is true about what is. Lies are therefore unreal precisely because they do not represent anything, only a false picture. The Word is the word of truth. Hatred is the denial of the solidarity among people which the rational creative principle makes necessary. Hatred is fragmentation and irrationality. It is a denial of the Word. For the rational principle – because it is true and brings light and life – is heartwarming, lovely, something we can depend upon.

I insist, this is not abstraction or fantasy. It is practical philosophy, commonsense. For just consider the reverse – consider what the consequences would be like if St John were wrong: we would be enjoined to believe that the sustaining power of the universe, the Word, the link between the past and the present which is one of the names of God, is darkness, ignorance, lies, hatred and death.

And that, of course, is just a contradiction in terms.

For no one could base a *language* (a Word) on lies: that would be self-defeating. No one could recommend hatred as a principle of human interaction – for the same reason. No one could reasonably prefer ignorance to understanding or nothing to something.

Only remember that the language in which this is expressed in St John and in the Creed is a metaphor, picture-language. That does not mean it is untrue, but that the meaning has to be interpreted and derived by means of the picture.

The doctrine of the Incarnation means, among other things, that what holds true for us holds true eternally. It means also that what we uphold as most lovely, lively and illuminating can be always guaranteed. God with us. Emmanuel. The Christmas hymns – hymns of the Incarnation – return to mind.

All right, so we have demythologised the doctrine of the Incarnation. We have shown that what is temporally most valuable, true and lovely is eternally so. But why all the emphasis on this one man Jesus? Why should he be singled out as the embodiment (Incarnation) of eternal truth?

The answer has nothing to do with magic and myths or abstractions, and everything to do with experience. For the eternal truth reveals itself episodically and progressively in history. That is to say, eternal truth is not static and abstract like Plato's Forms. It is constantly and consistently growing, developing and revealing more of itself like Aristotle's oak tree.

Let us go back to St Paul again on the road to Damascus. There was a blinding flash of revelation, certainty; but this was the culmination of much anguish and thought about the nature of Christ. Paul was a highly educated Jew. And Jewish tradition over two thousand years had developed the notion of the Son of God, the Messiah or Christ. What became indubitable to Paul the scholar, Paul the traditionalist steeped in the Scriptures, was that this man Jesus was the fulfilment of the prophecies, the expectation, of the Christ.

Here was the fulfilment of Isaiah, the 'man of sorrows and acquainted with grief' who was 'led as a lamb to the slaughter', who 'hath borne our griefs and carried our sorrows . . . wounded for our transgressions, bruised for our iniquities . . . and with his stripes we are healed'.

Tradition develops its own themes. St Paul, because he was steeped in the tradition of Jewish faith and messianic expectation, was able to go on and develop radically new – and yet entirely consistent – doctrines out of his experience. And so Christ was seen not only as the Suffering Servant prophesied by Isaiah, not only as the Righteous Branch from the House of David, but also as 'The New Adam' – the one who would reverse the consequences of Original Sin.

This is to say that, in the Gospel-writers as well as in St Paul, we see the whole weight of prophecy falling upon Jesus and those writers' experience of his life either at first hand or told to them by the earliest disciples. When they considered the life of Jesus of Nazareth against the whole background of their tradition, it simply became undeniable that here was the Christ. The point is this: *any other interpretation than the one they arrived at would have been less true to the historical evidence of two thousand years of Old Testament tradition and writing*.

We must also consider the non-biblical background to the proclamation that Christ is God incarnate. For Christianity is not just an efflorescence of Jewish tradition, but a synthesis between Jewish and Greek thought. The Middle East where Paul and the Gospel-writers lived was the melting pot of Western culture. The place was alive with philosophies, cults and religious sects: Stoics, Orphics, Epicureans, Mystery Religions and national gods. Among the most intelligent and informed people in Palestine and throughout the Jewish

dispersion in Asia Minor, two traditions prevailed: Rab-
binic Judaism – that is the style found in the parables
and pithy sayings in the gospels; and Greek thought –
notably the philosophies of Plato and Aristotle.

The Jewish tradition prophesied the Messiah or
Christ. Aristotle proclaimed that the world of ideas and
the world of matter were inseparably joined. Matthew,
Mark and Luke see Jesus as the fulfilment of the Jewish
tradition, while John sees him as the example of Greek
truth: the Word made flesh. Paul effects the synthesis.
For Paul, Jesus Christ is Messiah and Son of God,
Deliverer and Suffering Servant, and he is also the
Incarnation of what is eternally true: 'The Form of God'
(*Philippians* 2:6). No wonder his doctrine was – as he
himself confessed – a scandal to the Jews and foolish-
ness to the Greeks! It was nevertheless a creative fusion
of two traditions in the proclamation of a new idea – but
an idea embodied in a Person. That is the Incarnation.
God with us. The eternal truth manifested in its actual-
ity in the world of time and flux.

The next question is, of course, whether all this is
really true in the objective sense. This is a difficult issue
for our own times because we are obsessed with the idea
of objective truth – a concept we have derived from
scientific investigation. Our minds persuaded of the
objective truth that water boils at 100° centigrade and
that the air we breathe is four fifths nitrogen and one
fifth oxygen, we turn to the doctrine of the Incarnation
and require its verification in the same sense of the
phrase 'objective truth'.

It will not work like this. For scientific truth and
religious truth are quite different in kind. For a propo-
sition to be scientifically true, it must be verifiable in
terms which are independent of history. Water boiled

at 100° centigrade whether it boiled last night or last millennium. Religious truth, by contrast, is the creation of our experience, our tradition and cultural civilisation.

Let me offer one example: that of the Jewish experience as set down in the Old Testament and culminating in the Christological revelation of St Paul and the Gospel-writers. This story begins with the creation by God of a world which is good. It proceeds, by way of man's primeval disobedience, to the giving of the Law for our correction and guidance, through the admonishments and chastisements handed out by the prophets, to the realisation that man cannot save himself: that, therefore, if he is to be saved, God must take a hand in the saving; moreover, that this cannot be achieved by God at a transcendent distance, but must be accomplished by his coming to be with us as we are. I admit that this is an absurdly brisk history of the doctrine of the Incarnation, but it is roughly the way in which that doctrine arose. It was the distilled development of at least two thousand years of experience. It makes no sense to ask whether it is objectively true, any more than it makes sense to ask whether the Jews of the Old Testament and the early Christian believers were objectively true. All that can be said is that the religious story, based upon human experience in the Judeo-Hellenistic tradition, developed in the way it did.

I think we can say a little more: we can say that, if anyone had tried to develop the story in a different way, they would have done less than justice to the tradition and the experience. There have always been such people, of course, and they used to be known as heretics. Arius was one. But to call a man a heretic is not to despise him. Heretics are absolutely necessary to the forging of orthodoxy – that is, an authentic tradition. The Incarnation has become a part of living Christian tradition, whereas Arius, though intellectually admired, has been rejected.

When we ask whether the Incarnation is objectively true, then, we are asking the wrong question. All we can say is that *this* is the way our culture and tradition has developed – and not by accident, but by the most rigorous debate involving its best minds and, unfortunately but equally necessary, the wars of religion. We cannot reasonably ask for more than this: out of our experience has evolved our doctrine, our truth, our psychological and spiritual insight into what manner of people we are, and what constitutes our relationship with the cosmos.

I believe that this sort of truth is much to be preferred to the so-called 'objective truth'. The truths of science may be true, but they are impersonal. Religious truth is personal, located in the history and experience of a people and a culture – in a literature of spiritual struggle. That is to say, the doctrine of the Incarnation is not an abstraction – or a piece of the much-coveted and spurious 'objectivity' – but is itself incarnated in human experience.

Whatever heretics, ancient or modern, might honestly wish for, the Incarnation is the only story of our culture which can be consistently told; the only story that does full justice to our experience. It goes very deep into the soul of our culture, even creates that soul. For the Incarnation is not just a form of words, a doctrine, an opinion; it is emblazoned on the tangible world by the best minds of our era. We think of the Sistine Chapel or the C minor mass of Mozart. Of Giotto and Leonardo. Of the ethical characterisation of Dante's *Divine Comedy* or the novels of Dostoevsky and George Eliot.

These all start from the unspoken presupposition that the Incarnation is true, a fact of all our lives, a governing influence in the development of all that we are. We are as we are, and, being as we are, the story of Christ is the only one that does justice to the whole of our experience. For those who want 'objective truth', no doubt all this sounds very woolly, arty. I would reply that the art of religious expression is not mere ornament and adornment of the scientific world view – something to take our minds off napalm, the ozone layer and the bomb – but the very embodiment – Incarnation – of our experience, honed, sharpened and cast by thousands of years of critical, personal reflection.

This is what is meant by saying that the Incarnation – like the Resurrection – is a dogma. Not something dreamed up over liqueurs by some self-seeking prelate, but a concentration of truth into a few words which are basic to our culture in that they provide the rule by which other innovations, whether in art or religion, are judged. Dogma has a right to set itself up as that rule and that criterion, because it is the distilled expression of the experience of a whole civilisation over millennia. Four thousand years of consistent expression are not overturned in one sceptical night. On the basis of *what* (in any case) could any Westerner reject the doctrine of the Incarnation – since all his thought, in the words and artistic creations of our civilisation, are created and determined by that doctrine. *This is how it is with us*. To put this another way: if Christian civilisation has been in the wrong these last two thousand years, on the basis of *what* is it proposed that we begin to put it right?

But let us approach as near as we dare to the altar of scientific prejudice and the shrine of 'objective truth'. Let us ask again whether the Incarnation is true. Well, what do we mean by 'Incarnation'? Partly, we mean that certain qualities which we worship as divine were found in all their fullness in the man Jesus. So that, when we saw Jesus, we saw God: 'The Word was with God, and the Word was God.'

What were those qualities? Strength, intelligence, perseverance. A disregard for popularity. Compassion. Lucidity. So much love for his fellow men that he even prayed for those who were murdering him. Our faith says – via the doctrine of the Incarnation – that this is what the eternal God is like.

But is it true?

What we may reply is that it is the highest we have ever thought, and so it *ought* to be true. That if the word 'God' means anything to us, then it must mean at least this much. The doctrine of the Incarnation is born out of thousands of years of human suffering and reflection on that suffering. It is the best answer to our questions about God and man that we have ever come up with. There is nowhere else to begin, except with this doctrine. It is our backbone.

Finally, because Christianity is about ethics as well as metaphysics – because it is incarnated in *this* world – because it is about what we *do* as well as what we *believe* – we agree with the monk who said that belief is work. And so, if we believe that the Incarnation is true, we work to realise its glory in our own lives until we make it true.

5

The Truth of
the Resurrection

How can anyone believe in the Resurrection from the dead? After all, we live in a scientific world and we know that time must have a stop – that stories of resurrections and life after death belong to a more primitive age. Many modern theologians, and even a few bishops, urge us towards scepticism. For 'modern man' in his 'secular environment' surely the Resurrection of Jesus and the hope of eternal life must have, at best, a mythological or metaphorical significance?

He could not have simply risen from the dead, could he? And we know, do we not, that as natural creatures we shall die one day, and that will be the end of us?

Resurrection and life after death would be a miracle. And the influential modern theologian Rudolf Bultmann has said, 'You can't believe in miracles in an age of electric light and the wireless.'

More recently, David Jenkins, sometime Bishop of Durham, has told us that the Resurrection was not 'a conjuring trick with bones' but that it was something spiritual. What, then, are we to think? Did Jesus rise from the dead, or not? Do we have any realistic hope of a Resurrection to eternal life? These are enormously complicated questions, but they may turn out to be a little less complicated if we can begin by clearing up a few common misconceptions and ordinary nonsense.

First, the Resurrection of Jesus was not the resuscitation of a corpse. No one – not even God – breathed new life into a dead body.

We know this for certain.

We know it because, in the Resurrection stories in the Gospels, the risen Jesus does not appear like a man of flesh and blood. Well, sometimes he does: as when he asks Thomas to prove he is not a ghost by putting his fingers into his palms and his hand into his side; or when he asks his disciples to give him something to eat. But what are we to make of the story of the walk to Emmaus on Easter evening when it was said that his disciples did not know him? How could they not know someone with whom they had spent the last three years of their lives – unless the Resurrection body was something different from the body of his flesh?

On that occasion, it was said that Jesus 'vanished' out of their sight. Flesh-and-blood bodies do not vanish.

On another occasion, Jesus passes through a wall. Bodies of flesh do not do such things.

Religious controversies feed on ignorance. The Bible nowhere says that the Resurrection was a simple resuscitation. It insists, in all four Gospels, that the Resurrection was a reality. It did happen. So what happened?

It is a mystery. This is not an evasion of the issue. It is only to say that, if the Resurrection happened, it was the manifestation of something other-worldly. And the language of this world cannot adequately describe a world beyond this world. If heaven could be described in earthly terms, it would not be heaven but only a sort of conceivable utopia. Politics would have supplanted religion.

Whatever happened, the four Gospels are certain that something happened. And that something was that Jesus appeared to his disciples again after the crucifixion. At least, that is what is said.

Perhaps the disciples, disappointed and dejected, made the whole thing up? But it does not seem likely that such inspiration as caused them to preach his Resurrection among all nations should have sprung from a lie. So maybe they were mistaken? Perhaps they dreamt the whole thing, as a kind of wish-fulfilment, an antidote to their disappointment? But there are so many accounts of Resurrection appearances. It was no one-off. Jesus appears to many of the disciples on many different occasions. And often the accounts are tales told against the disciples – how they did not recognise him, how they would not believe, did not know what to think or do. In short, the stories of the Resurrection appearances are full of just the sort of confusion and bewilderment as we might expect, just supposing for a minute that the event had actually occurred. If anyone had wanted to invent the story – as in the case of a cast-iron alibi – they would have been careful that in all points the story agreed with itself: no contradictions; no inconsistencies. But the Resurrection stories are full of contradictions and inconsistencies. That is one of the main reasons for believing them to be true. They strike us as hastily delivered stuff of astounding experience and not as a contrived account by megalomaniacs and liars.

The most commonly expressed argument against the Resurrection is that, as it were, these things simply do not happen. The Resurrection is alleged to be something that no sane, modern person could possibly believe – 'in an age of electric light and the wireless'. This is simply a prejudice. Notice, no reason is offered against the Resurrection except a blind assumption that it could not happen – because *these sorts of things do not happen*. This is a modernistic prejudice. It is very widespread and influential. There is, however, no reason why we should pay more attention to a modern prejudice than we would pay to an ancient one.

Moreover, the modern prejudice against the Resurrection is based on science – or at least on pseudo-science and the so-called 'scientific world-view'. Not all scientists are atheists, of course, but the scientific world-view is one-worldly. That is to say, it rejects the idea that events in this world can be affected by agencies and powers in another world. The scientific prejudice is against metaphysics and any notion of transcendence. It will not allow miracles. It asserts that all events which occur in this world can, at least in principle, be explained in terms of this world.

The 'scientific world-view' believes this because it has had some success in explaining why *some* events occur. The leap of prejudice makes it claim that because *some* events can be explained in this-worldly terms, then *all* events can be so explained. Like all prejudices, this 'scientific' prejudice is irrational. It is reductive. That is, it rules out certain possible causes of events as if these causes were impossible. We have got so used to this 'scientific' prejudice – it has become part of our mental furniture – that we take it for granted. We have come to regard a prejudice, a demonstrable irrationality, as if it were no prejudice but a highly rational and genuinely scientific fact.

This outlook permeates all life and areas of thought. So, for instance, modern psychology ('psychology' based on a Greek word for 'soul') does not believe that we have souls or even minds. Human activity is described as *behaviour* by *organisms* that do not have choices but only *exhibit behaviour* as a result of physical *stimuli* and the rules of *classical* and *operant conditioning*. This is not the place for a detailed study of *Behaviourism*. I mention it only as an example of how the 'scientific' prejudice has invaded every area of thought and discussion about the human condition. With what result? With the result that the modern psychologist cannot talk about those human feelings which we have always held to be our deepest feelings, those that we would regard as distinctively human. For it makes no sense to speak of an organism having faith, behaving heroically or falling in love. Thus the language and method of modern psychology is subhuman. We are *organisms* or *information systems* without souls, choices or a significant will. We are machines in which there are no ghosts.

It is a scandal that, although Behaviourism has been frequently and convincingly discredited, it is still taught as the basis of psychological understanding in most Western universities. Behaviourism excludes ninety-five per cent of the history of our culture: all those poems and pictures about love and death, joy, despair and hope – and, of course, transcendence, God. Notice also that it reduces ethics and morality to mere convention. For, if it makes no sense to speak of *organisms* having choices, it certainly makes no sense to speak of their making *moral* choices.

Arthur Koestler asked the question, in his famous critique of behaviourism in *The Ghost in the Machine*, if behaviourism is so thoroughly discredited intellectually and philosophically, why say any more about it? In short, 'Why flog a dead horse?' Because, says Koestler, 'Never did a dead horse have such a powerful kick.' Quite. As I pointed out, it is still the basis of most psychological teaching in our universities where the human insights of real psychologists such as Freud and Jung are regarded as merely fanciful.

The scientific prejudice not only kills off traditional psychological and spiritual insights, it destroys our civilisation and culture because it separates *objects* from their *meaning*. What, for instance, is the point of a cathedral for an age which has no room for transcendence, for God? Well, we can see what point there is in them: they have become attractions for the blundering tourists to gawp at; monuments to a dead culture and a dead God.

And now what do they believe instead? Behaviourism and the scientific prejudice which defines miracles as logically impossible and says there is no Resurrection.

Similarly, a plainsong Mass was not meant to be a concert performance, but an integral part of an activity called *worship*. If there is no transcendence, what is the meaning of 'worship', and hence of the plainsong Mass? Answer: it no longer has any meaning. It is only a piece of cultural flotsam.

The scientific prejudice denies the meaning of anything that originated in the pre-scientific age: miracles, Masses, prayers, cathedrals and so on. But it preserves the shell – the art works, the buildings, the outward and visible signs of what were once taken to be spiritual truths. The best that can be said of our scientific age is that it is acting in a decadent way when it preserves art and artefacts while denying their meaning. It is a schizophrenic attitude. No wonder the modern world is dissociated.

The scientific prejudice is itself a decadent form of religion. It is an ersatz, pseudo religion. I had better say what I mean by the word 'religion'. It is that thing which is held to be true at the deepest level. It is the thing, the touchstone, by which everything else is judged and measured. Religion is what is most basic, normative. But there are different varieties of religion, and I do not simply mean Christianity, Buddhism, Islam etc.

There is biblical religion and traditional Christianity. And there is modern, 'scientific' religion.

Traditional Christianity is a form of thought, feeling and expression which embraces God, angels and men, human life from before the cradle to after the grave. It has always believed that there are two worlds: The Kingdom of this world and the Kingdom of God. Moreover, God has created this world out of nothing and, from time to time, he acts decisively and miraculously in it. The main miracles are the Incarnation and the Resurrection.

Traditional Christianity holds these things to be true, to be logically consistent and to be the measure of truth by which everything else must be judged.

The modern scientific religion believes that there is one world and that miracles, along with all other supernatural incursions into the monist cosmos, simply do not happen – because they *cannot* happen. These events are ruled out, defined as impossible before the discussion begins. The scientific religion is thus itself an act of faith – some would say a posture of arrogance. For it nowhere disproves the existence of the transcendent world; it merely asserts that such a world is not going to be so much as considered in the way it thinks about events. God is not disproved, only denied and disowned.

Why be so iconoclastic? Partly because ideas are not the subject of disinterestedness except in the most Socratic settings, and they generally involve a bid for power of one kind or another. Science claims to be able to explain – at least in principle – all phenomena. It believes it has the foolproof *method* with which to do this. When it comes to God, science – along with Laplace – 'has no need of that hypothesis'. Interesting that science should even remake God in its own image by so speaking of him as a *hypothesis*.

Shakespeare says: 'There are more things in heaven and earth than are dreamed of in your philosophy.' Science outlaws heaven from the start. It regards the transcendent world, God, as irrelevant. I call science a religious disposition because it is just an act of faith – an act of faith by a discipline which spends much of its time denying the possibility of acts of faith. Science – as religion – simply claims that God and a transcendent world are redundant as explanatory forces. God is surplus to requirements.

The last three hundred years have seen theology in retreat while science has advanced, carrying all before it. Remarkable that theology in the Middle Ages was called 'the queen of sciences'. The final irony is that theology has only survived as an academic discipline in the West by itself assuming the scientific method: the Graf-Wellhausen *theory* of Old Testament authorship; St Paul's epistles subjected to 'computer-verification'. Naturalistic explanations invented to account for miracles which are allegedly incredible in the modern age.

The most recent confirmation of the judgement that today even the Christian faith has to fit the measure of science was in a talk by Dr Charles Elliott on Radio Four's *Thought For the Day* when he described the Resurrection of Christ as 'a plausible hypothesis'.

When the events of the Christian religion are discussed in the language of science, then it is a religion no longer. This is because it is no longer basic. Instead the scientific analysis, method and language are what has become basic. One religion is replaced by another.

In actual practice, the development has not been as extreme as this. The Christian religion has not been entirely abandoned, only set within the scientific-historical framework of the modern world-view, and the original Christian stories are interpreted in a demythologised and non-supernaturalist sense. The new interpretative language has replaced the authority of Scripture and the teaching of the Church. We have so gradually and yet so fully accomplished this replacement that we hardly ever recognise that a shift has taken place at all. And the Resurrection is nowhere disproved by science; it has only become the casualty of a materialistic prejudice which we foolishly regard as scientific and therefore authoritative. Along with Professor Bultmann, we are only too ready to suppose that the Resurrection is unbelievable 'in an age of electric light and the wireless' – and still more unbelievable in an age of spaceflight and microprocessors.

Ironically, the materialist prejudice is enjoying its greatest success at just the same time as real science – and particularly sub-atomic physics – claims that the world is not best explained by materialistic hypotheses. Modern physics is more spiritual than modern theology.

This, however, is only an aside. For it would be a mistake for Christian believers to draw comfort from a particular fashion in science. Fashions change. It is as mistaken for the Christian believer to take comfort from what he perceives as friendly science as it is for him to be discouraged by science in its more hostile periods – the nineteenth century, for example. For science and Christianity are different languages. Their worlds are thus radically different. The Resurrection is not, as Dr Elliott believes, a 'plausible hypothesis'; it is a dogma, a teaching based on another authority altogether from that upon which hypotheses are based.

The question which I cannot escape is that of whether biblical and ecclesiastical language and tradition says more of what is true in the human sense than the scientific language says. If it is a choice between the wonderful order of angels and men, principalities and powers corresponding to our deepest feelings and another order which talks of 'the empty organism . . . stimulus and response . . . conditioning both classical and operant . . .' – then I cannot but choose the first way. The biblical and Church traditions of that first way *cannot* be discussed at all in the terminology of the second way – no, not even as 'plausible hypotheses'. How can an organism which (even according to its proposers) has no soul, mind or consciousness but which is only a bundle of stimuli and responses begin to evaluate the significance of church music, the beauty of the cathedrals, the being of angels and the existence of God?

I said that there are no disinterested systems of ideas except the lofty aspirations of Socrates. But perhaps so-called 'pure science' aspires to disinterestedness? At least it claims to do so. I am thinking particularly of physics and astronomy, or of mathematics. However, our modern culture is not shaped by pure science or disinterestedness of any kind, but by the materialistic prejudice – by technology – which wants only to make us more comfortable in our indulgences. If the image of the man in Bunyan's time was 'the pilgrim', in today's world it is as 'the consumer' that he is most readily recognised. Materialistic comforts are the universal aim. Indeed, in a world which rejects what is transcendent and spiritual, what other comforts could there be?

The Resurrection of Jesus depends upon the existence of God. God is ignored as irrelevant in our age. He is not part of our mental furniture. His existence has not been disproved, though the prejudice behaves as if it has been. I maintain that the existence of God is a reasonable and consistent belief. As Francis Bacon said in *Of Atheism*, 'I had rather believe all the fables in the Legend, and the Talmud and the Alcoran than that this universal frame is without a mind.'

Of course, I am aware that those scientific psychologists who deny the existence of the human mind think differently. What they think *with* is another question! I cannot believe that logic and mathematics, language and orderly thought, originated in what is less than orderly. The clay does not mould the potter. 'The fool hath said in his heart, There is no God.' The idea that man, after his short history in the cosmos, is the measure of all things seems like arrogance to me. On the other hand, systematic theologians from St Augustine in the fourth century to St Thomas Aquinas in the thirteenth, to Bernard Lonergan in the twentieth, have taught that the world is of a piece and that the lowliest objects and systems of life are part of a continuum which leads upwards and into God. These teachings are coherent and human. They are more in keeping with our ordinary experience of the world – and also our understanding of our own creativity – than the world of the empty organism.

But, in the end, the existence of God cannot be proved in the scientific sense any more than the Resurrection can be proved. I have tried to show that even to attempt such a proof is a sort of category-mistake – it is to apply one language to the domain of another.

At any rate, I am only determined to show that it is not unreasonable to believe in God. There is nothing contradictory in the claim that he exists. That is to say, the first condition for belief in the Resurrection has been met: the existence of God cannot be ruled out. In a more exalted way, this is the case made by the New Testament itself, of course: that it is God who raised Jesus from the dead.

Secondly, we need to be able to accept the existence and reality of a spiritual world if we are to believe in the Resurrection. Fashionable prejudice rejects spirituality but then discovers it can do so only at irretrievable cost to itself. For we need to talk about whom and what we love. We need to express what it is that our will chooses to do. These are mental and spiritual acts. To deny them means not only that we deny a spiritual world *out there*, but that we give up our humanity. For a humanity without choices and without the capacity to love – or, for that matter, to hate, to fear, to believe and even to disbelieve – is no humanity. We cannot even begin to talk about ourselves or anything else until we admit a non-material, spiritual dimension to our lives. Of course it makes only metaphorical sense to speak of the spiritual reality as 'beyond the sky' or 'outside space and time', and sometimes metaphors can be as much a hindrance as a help.

Speaking plainly, then, our human experience and the very faculty of speech and thought demonstrate the existence of a spiritual world. It is not infinitely remote, but part of us – part of the undeniable truth about us. When we experience awe and reverence – 'holy fear' – or beauty and tenderness that touches our very centre, we know also that, as well as being a part of us, the spiritual world is beyond us. And that is why we need metaphors – to help us express what we (spiritually – humanly) need to express but what is beyond ordinary expression.

We must be careful not to separate the material world and the spiritual world. They are bound up together. This is obvious. For the spiritual faculty by which we live requires something tangible for us to love. Similarly, choices are made between *things*.

The essential oneness of the spiritual and the material is summed up in the profoundest Christian metaphor: God With Us. And it is visualised in thousands of pictures, pieces of music, poems and hymns – none better than:

> 'Thou who art beyond the farthest
> Mortal eye can scan,
> Can it be that thou regardest
> Songs of sinful man?
> Can we know that thou art near us,
> And wilt hear us?
> Yea, we can.'

Francis Pott's great hymn begins with angel voices and goes on to celebrate the creative power of flesh-and-blood human beings which allows us to share the angelic vision. 'Angels and men constituted in a wonderful order,' as it says in the Prayer Book Collect: it means that what is spiritual belongs to the same reality as what is material. It is true (though not very poetic) to say that spirit and matter are two aspects of one and the same thing. Deny either aspect and our world of experience falls apart and we end up talking nonsense. Split the two and our theology and thought become schizophrenic, unreal.

This is the perspective by which we perceive the Resurrection. It is a dramatic affirmation of the continuing oneness of matter and spirit. I repeat, it is not the mere resuscitation of a corpse. A resuscitation of that kind would not be good news for the generations of mankind which have been since the time of Christ and whose bodies have either completely disappeared into the dust of the earth or have been consumed by fire in the crematorium. Still, a faith which declares 'ashes to ashes, dust to dust' also proclaims 'I believe in the Resurrection from the dead'.

How can this be? St Paul, groping for a satisfactory explanation – one that avoids the conclusion that the resurrected Jesus was either a resuscitated corpse or a ghost – tells us that he was a 'soma-pneumatikon', that is 'a spiritual body'. Moreover, Jesus is 'the first-fruits of them that slept'. And we, when we die, shall be made like him.

This means that our personal identity – though not the present materiality of our bodies – will survive death. Death is a trauma but not a finality. 'We shall know as we are known,' says Paul to the Corinthians. And we are known and recognised by our appearance, some sort of body. At the Resurrection we shall be given – as Jesus was given – a new body, a body suitable for the life of the world to come.

This body will be recognisably *our* body, as Jesus' body was recognisably his – though, as we see by his appearance on the road to Emmaus and his appearance to Mary when she first took him for the gardener, this recognition may take a little time.

Why, except to the most hidebound materialist or the most bigoted pseudo-scientist, should this sound implausible? Only the denial of the existence of God (which is arrogance) and the denial of the spiritual dimension of reality (which is a contradiction in terms) make the Resurrection sound implausible. Once the prejudice in favour of atheism and the other prejudice in favour of materialism are set aside, then belief in the Resurrection seems natural and reasonable.

It was not 'a conjuring trick with bones'. In one sense Bishop Jenkins was right. The Resurrection needs to be considered theologically – that is, we must see what it means in the whole context of biblical faith. It means that what God has created can never be destroyed. God may create a new heaven and a new earth, but these will not be entirely new. They will be continuous with the old heaven and the old earth. That is why they retain the same names 'heaven' and 'earth'. He may put a new heart in us, but it will be recognisably *our* heart. That is why it is said to be put in *us*. He will give us a new, Resurrection, body but it will embody *us*. It will reveal and express our personality, our identity, in a way that a ghost or a resuscitated corpse never could.

When all is said and done, the most lucid and wonderful description of the Resurrection is given not in the Gospel fragments which speak of Jesus' brief and puzzling appearances on and after the first Easter Sunday, but in St Paul's Letter to the Corinthians, Chapter 15.

It is instructive to note that it is this description of our final destiny, which is with Christ, that is prescribed to be read at services for The Burial of the Dead.

6

The Femininity of God and Man

When we think of God we inevitably reveal the structure of our own minds, for the doctrine of God is the theological reflection of the mind of humankind. Theology and psychology are nothing more than the inside and outside of the same thing – our humanness.

And when we think about the issue of feminism and the place of women we must begin with humanity's reflections on the nature of God. For the entire history of the Judaeo-Christian civilisation continues to exert a powerful influence over all our notions of woman.

The Judaeo-Christian civilisation is rampantly masculine. The first stories told to our children are full of manly, warlike deeds: man the servant of God; man as God's prophet; man the great, the divinely inspired leader of the tribe or the nation. The archetypal heroes of our tradition are Abraham, Jacob, Moses and Joshua and their sons, the great kings David and Solomon; the prophets Amos, Hosea, Isaiah, Jeremiah and Ezekiel. The character of John the Baptist is the last word in machismo in his coat of camel's hair and living on locusts and wild honey; not to mention Jesus himself, the new Joshua, the Messiah and Son of Man; St Paul, who thought that women should be quiet in church.

All these men worshipped the one God, the Lord, the God of armies who was known for his wrath, for his warlike deeds on behalf of his people, for his leading the fierce tribes of Israel with a mighty hand and an outstretched arm. This is the God known to English readers of the Bible as the Lord. His name in the ancient languages always connotes masculine power: he is God Almighty, God of the Mountains, God whose spirit lurks in the desert places where it whips up the sands into a fury. This God is in storm and tempest, in clouds and earthquakes; he pours fire and brimstone down on the sinful cities of the plain. In the Gospel of St Matthew it is this same God who sits on his throne in judgement, separating the sheep from the goats, having the power to cast erring souls into the nethermost hell.

Genesis says that God made man in his own image. From the theological point of view, that is absolutely correct, orthodox. But from the psychological viewpoint it is man who makes God in man's own image. This is necessarily so, since all perceptions and conceptions, all doctrines and image-making, are expressed by means of language: and language is a human creation. So God who inhabits the highest heaven is thought of in terms which owe their origin to the psychological make-up and political organisation of terrestrial man. In the patriarchal world of the Old Testament, women are regarded as inferior to men. When they do get a chance to move to the centre of the stage, they are often shown as contributing to man's downfall: so it is Eve who, seduced by the serpent, issues the fatal temptation to Adam; and it is Sarah, Abraham's wife, who gets her husband into trouble by laughing at the angel of the Lord.

The Ten Commandments prohibit all forms of idolatry, but the Hebrew prophets particularly condemned those who worshipped the fertility goddesses of the Canaanite plain. God was one. God was to be obeyed. And God was male, a man of war. But this onesidedness, this extreme obsession with masculinity, could not be maintained for ever, despite the political and sociological forces operating in its favour. For a true understanding of human psychology shows that even the manliest man has his feminine side and that women share many of the male qualities. This understanding has been demonstrated in our own century by C. G. Jung and it is supported by information gathered from genetic research. The androgynous nature of mankind has been attested throughout history, and it is a profound and persistent theme in most of civilisation's great stories and myths.

Even the Old Testament cannot perpetually depict God as wholly masculine, divorced from all femininity. In Proverbs, Ecclesiastes and the Book of Wisdom the Lord God has a consort whose name is Wisdom. The word used is the Greek 'Sophia', a feminine noun. Man is urged in these books to seek wisdom as if involved in an act of courtship: from a psychological perspective this is the signal for man to pay attention to his intuitive, feminine qualities and so harmonise his nature by integrating its different aspects. In the book of the prophet Hosea, God himself begins to exhibit a quality of tenderness: he is portrayed as the loving husband of an unfaithful wife – Israel. The redemption of the erring, harlot nation Israel in Hosea's book comes about through a union of masculine and feminine aspects. And, according to Jung, this is an image of what must happen in the soul or psyche of every man (and every woman too) if he is to become whole, integrated, balanced. Or, as the older theological language puts it, redeemed and saved.

Of course, man is stubborn, and he often resists the way to his own integration. He denies his feminine side. We see this in many forms throughout history. It is there in St Paul's misogyny and in St Augustine's fear of women which he translated into a furious and fanatical insistence on the overriding merits of virginity. In his book *City of God*, St Augustine goes so far as to permit sexual relations – as long as the participants derive no enjoyment from these acts! It is there, too, in the witch-hunts of the Middle Ages and in the Church's obsession with sexual sins – even when orthodoxy itself insists that the sins of the flesh are not as serious or as destructive as the sins of the spirit, such as pride, which, in biblical mythology, was at the source of Satan's original disobedience. But even in our own supposedly liberal age, it is still sexual offences which attract the strongest disapproval: we do not hear of men as having been dismissed from the church choir on account of excessive pride! But let a churchgoer be a discovered adulterer and see how quickly and how fiercely denunciation and ostracism ensue.

The life and work of Jesus did much to restore the balance between masculine and feminine aspects. Women were little better than slaves in the man's world of first-century Palestine. But Jesus went out of his way to associate with them. Not all of these women were entirely respectable: it is widely believed, for example, that Mary Magdalene either was or had been a prostitute. In St John's Gospel, Jesus refuses to condemn the woman taken in adultery – 'in the very act'. It is women who stand by the cross when the manly disciples have fled to save their own skins. Women anoint his body for the burial. And women are the first witnesses to the Resurrection. 'The first day of the week cometh Mary Magdalene early, when it was yet dark, unto the sepulchre.'

Christian teaching about the Incarnation and the virgin birth represents a great advance on old masculine, Jewish mentality. For here the great masculine God, the high and mighty Lord of Lords, the only ruler of princes, depends for his greatest revelation of himself upon the willing co-operation of a young Jewish girl. We wonder how St Paul squared his anti-feminism with the tradition of divine partnership with woman as revealed by the doctrine of the virgin birth. Perhaps we wonder also, in an age when bishops are fond of airing their doubts about the virgin birth, whether their denials do not tell us more about themselves and their own unconscious psychological rejection of femininity in religion than about the alleged facts concerning Our Lady.

In the history of the Church and of Christian spirituality, there have been many women who were not content to remain passive but who exercised powers of spiritual insight and leadership, founding religious orders and institutions, even preaching the word of God and, in the archetypal character of Joan of Arc, leading armies. Mother Julian of Norwich, in her visions out of which she compiled 'Revelations of Divine Love', claimed that God is our mother as well as our father. And the frequently androgynous character of angels in Christian art and iconography shows a desire to represent spiritual reality as composed of both masculine and feminine aspects. That is a theological representation.

Its psychological correlative is to be found in the very down-to-earth truth that, in his inner life no less than in his outward behaviour, man requires woman for his completion. And she requires him.

Jung divides man's soul or psyche into two parts: conscious and unconscious. Man's consciousness is masculine. His unconscious is feminine. Jung calls the unconscious feminine aspect the anima. This is a very powerful image, literally pregnant with meaning. For it is the anima – meaning that which gives life, enlivens – which urges man on to deeds of bravery and to the creative expression of his true self. The best way to envisage the work of the anima is to move away from the abstract terminology of analytical psychology and to see the actual personification of the feminine principle in the great and abiding works of Western literature and culture. Those stories of gods and goddesses are not just fairytales. They are not so trivially dismissed. For the tales we tell reveal what manner of person we are.

In the growth and integration of our personalities, conscious and unconscious aspects must develop together in a mutually creative relationship. And, just as the conscious, observable boy-man must progress from childishness, in experience and maturity, to the full stature of manhood, so his unconscious aspect must develop too. We may catalogue man's development in stages like Shakespeare's seven ages of man: baby, child, youth, soldier, lover, accomplished adult and wise old man. The unconscious aspect, the anima, or woman-within, goes through a similar process of maturing and transformation from weakness to perfection. This process can be fascinatingly observed in the great myths and poems of our civilisation.

Her history parallels the development of the objective woman. First she is seen in all those stories of childhood innocence. This is the anima pre-puberty when, though she may evoke images of a childlike, paradisaical exist-ence, she is yet unawakened, impotent, unamoured. Images are of Eliot's 'children in the apple tree' – boy and girl (conscious and unconscious forces) existing together in a paradisaical, timeless world which does not yet know the ecstasy and the burden of sexual union. Usually in the paradisaical myths, the heavenly children do not work. Nothing is achieved. All is simply given. Work and progress begin with the traumatic events of arousal and intercourse. This symbolises the conscious and unconscious forces first becoming aware of each other and realising that mutual co-operation, though painful, is absolutely necessary. As C. H. Sisson wrote, this sexual union is not just what the 'rutting stag knows; it is to take Eve's apple and lose the paradisaical look'.

This is the transition from the pre-sexual world of childhood when male and female personalities co-operate – but without knowing their true adult nature and purpose – to the adult world of sexual initiation. The first stirrings of sexual arousal tell us who we are and what our purpose is. The symbolism is explicit in the Genesis story: we eat of the tree of knowledge. And in the biblical Hebrew, the word for knowledge is the same as that for the sex act. This is also the stage when the anima becomes temptress. Eve tempts Adam and he succumbs. But this is not a story found only in the Hebrew Bible. It is there too in Babylonian and other Near-Eastern myths. It is found in Greek culture in the story of the erotic Sirens, the temptresses who would lure Ulysses and all sailors on to the rocks. It is there in the romantic legends about wood-nymphs and the Lorelei who charm men to distraction.

Some feminists object to this description of the anima because they see it as necessarily showing woman in a poor light, putting all the blame on her for man's ills. In fact, their apprehension is quite needless. Man must fall in order to rise, that is to become a whole, integrated human being. That is the message of all those myths about Sirens and Temptresses. And the balance is ultimately redressed for, as we shall see, woman who is responsible for man's downfall is also the cause of his final redemption – a religious way of talking about his full maturity and the integration of his personality.

The image of the Temptress did not fade with the passing of ancient or classical culture. She is there in Hollywood, in the femme fatale, in every Siren and Temptress from 'the It-Girl' to Marilyn Monroe and the sexy Madonna (a very revealing title, in the context of the psychological-religious understanding of man's sexual and personal development!) The archetype of the Temptress in modern and popular culture can be well seen in works such as Alban Berg's opera 'Lulu', in Joseph von Sternberg's famous film 'The Blue Angel' and in Monroe's exasperating, fascinating role in 'Seven Year Itch'. There are more common examples in the pouting, posturing femmes fatales in 'Dallas' and 'Dynasty' as well as in the models who smile at men from the various page threes of daily tabloids. She is She: 'She who must be obeyed': Desire(e).

If a man is to achieve proper maturity, he must learn to leave behind the stage of sexual enchantment symbolised and represented by the Temptress, the Siren and the Lorelei. He must learn a proper perspective, a sense of adjustment to the world's realities. That is, he must acquire wisdom: wisdom, as we have seen, is personified in our cultural tradition as Sophia, the consort of God. Man is made, says scripture, in the image of God. So man, developing according to the divine pattern, must find that balance in the mature relationship between his consciousness and his anima that is expressed in the theological picture of the Lord with his consort Sophia. In external, objective terms, the anima-as-Sophia stage is personified in a man's relationship with his wife, which, it is to be hoped, still retains a sexual element but which puts sex into the context of a practical commitment to daily tasks, to working out a life together not so much in the heat and rush of the early sexual experiences, but in the shared life of mutual responsibility.

From girl-child to Temptress and Sophia, the anima as a man's unconscious develops in a positive, creative way. The man learns about his inwardness, and his inwardness gives him power – literally inspires, animates, him – so that he can continue to make progress towards full integration of the personality: to what in the older religious language was called salvation and redemption. The anima-as-Sophia stage may also be seen as the stage of the wife or companion. And the archetypal expression of the couple is not, at this stage, the erotic coupling of Faust and Gretchen, Tristan and Isolde or Romeo and Juliet: it is the mature stage of the wifely companion – what the Bible calls 'helpmeet' – personified by such as Dante and Beatrice on their worldly-spiritual pilgrimage.

This is the period of marriage. Theologically, it can be represented as marriage between the Lord and his people Israel, as in Hosea; sociologically, it corresponds to the institution of marriage as prescribed by society;

psychologically, it is the partnership and growing union between the conscious and unconscious aspects of the personality. We are talking about the very structure of the human personality – an older age would have used the word 'soul', which is, in any case, the word for the Latin 'anima' – so we should not expect images and representations of this universal condition to be restricted to orthodox theology and religious or secular high art. We are talking about every man's story. So, as in the examples from popular literature and films of the Temptress or *femme fatale*, we see in those same sources popular personifications of the companion. There are, for instance, the exciting stories of the opening up of the West in the USA: the waggon trains were driven by the heroes who were always supported by the wives, 'the womenfolk'. It is the image of the pilgrimage. When the couple as partners are attacked by hostile forces, they drive their waggons into a ring. The ring or circle, like the wedding ring, is the symbol of perfection, completion.

The final personification of the anima is as Virtue itself. Archetypally, this is seen clearest in our Judeo-Christian tradition in the person of the Blessed Virgin Mary. Because of her obedience, her perfect virtue, she becomes, according to traditional doctrine, the Mother of God, God-bearer.

Now at last the circle is complete. Scripture says, 'As in Adam all men die, so in Christ shall all be made alive.' The feminine counterparts in the masculine economy are, of course, Eve and Mary. As man was seduced by woman, so he is also saved by her. None of this is meant to cast a slur on particular women, and the feminist antagonism to the anima-psychology is, in my opinion, misplaced. I have only described psychological

processes as they actually occur and as they are pictured
in the art and literature of our culture and civilisation.
Those myths and legends are not trivial. They tell the
truth. They are our story. The circle is completed. Man
who falls because of Eve is raised because of Mary. A
new man is born – the Christchild – and the process is
begun all over again in the iconography of religious
symbolism and in the life of every man. The anima is
both good and bad, creative and destructive, just as the
conscious mind is also good and bad, capable of issuing
both blessings and curses.

Religious stories as found in the Bible are the basic
raw material by which a civilisation understands itself.
It was well said that every culture writes its poetic epics
at the beginning of its course. All that follows is an
attempt to tell the old story in new words. And the many
stories that are told serve to personify in exciting and
pictorial style the endlessly repeated programme of
man's inner development, his moral and spiritual
pilgrimage. How could things be otherwise? A mystery
which does not reveal some truth about us is always
rejected as uninteresting. We find certain stories
eternally fascinating, for they put into images the most
profound spiritual-psychological truths about what it is
to be a human being. And our various re-tellings of
primitive myth and saga are not mere repetition: each
new tale is itself, told in the cultural garb, in the
thought-forms and language of a particular historical
time and place. I will give some examples from so-called
'high' and 'popular' art of different ages. We should
not despise the popular versions, for they are the
means by which the many participate in the
understanding which high art has traditionally
mediated to the few.

The Romantic Age's reworking of the Bible's picturing of man's craving for wholeness, integration of the personality and salvation is to be found in Goethe's Faust. Here is the man, the hero, Everyman, who encounters his anima in all her various guises. He meets Gretchen as a child, loves her as a Siren and even kills her. But at the end of his life she appears as an angel from heaven to redeem him. She is Virtue personified. Grace. The story is wonderfully and evocatively told. And it is gloriously translated into musical terms in the 'Symphony Number Eight' by Gustav Mahler. This ends with the appearance of the heavenly choir who, in Goethe's words, give musical expression to the story of man's salvation:

> 'All things transitory
> Are as symbols sent;
> Earth's insufficiency
> Here finds fulfilment;
> Here the ineffable
> Wins life through love
> The Endless Woman-Soul [i.e. the anima]
> Leads us above.'

It should be said that the anima is one. She has many guises, but she herself is a unity. This means that in all the later stages of her development she yet contains the earlier ones. This is also the important difference between caricature and real character. The mature woman occasionally reveals the child or the Temptress in her. This is the undeniable principle of continuity in the development of human personality which raises human beings above the level of mere mechanism, mere organism – so beloved of the inhuman behavioural sciences – and makes life really lively (erotic) and immediate, tangible, not ghostly or abstract. Shakespeare's phrase 'too solid/sullied flesh' comes to mind.

All those fairytales about the Prince who hacks his way through the dense wood to find his Princess (his anima, his soulmate) tell the same story of each man's pilgrimage of self-discovery through the integration of his female aspects. And the story repeats itself in suitable technological garb in our own age in films such as *Star Wars* and even in the popular television series *Dr Who*. This is not fanciful. We must not be surprised when popular art gives expression to the story of Everyman. Indeed, what else should we expect any human storytelling to do except tell us something about the storytellers – ourselves?

The character Dr Who is a modern technological variant on the ancient gnostic Redeemer figure who comes from the supernatural world, armed with his secret knowledge and magic potions and powers to banish evil and right the terrestrial world of all wrongs. This figure was very popular in Middle-Eastern theology and mythology in the first few centuries AD. Now, in the sci-fi mode, Dr Who does just the same in our era. He is a Lord of Time or Time-Lord who comes from a world that is beyond time. He too brings his superior knowledge, his Tardis or machine which can transcend time and his many other magical gadgets. Like the gnostic Redeemer, he finds himself up against evil powers and principalities, spiritual wickedness in high places. Dr Who, over thirty years of programmes, always had a female assistant. It is marvellously supportive of the idea of the universality of the anima figure that, in a popular series like this one, the assistant should develop and change precisely according to the sequence of the anima's development in classic spirituality, mythology and human personality. At first she was a little child, Sarah. Then she became the savage Temptress, Leela. The next Incarnation was into the virtuous companion, Romana. And the final stage was the elevation of Romana to the rank of Time-Lady, so that she became the equal of the Doctor, the contemporary Incarnation of the gnostic Redeemer. Since this pattern of the anima's development is a universal phenomenon, we should not be in the least surprised to find it occurring wherever stories are told. It is not usually a conscious manipulation of symbolism by the writer but an eruption into consciousness of undeniable unconscious contents.

Jung has much to say about the most popular of all personifications of divine femininity: the doctrine of the assumption of the Blessed Virgin into heaven. This was long believed by the mass of ordinary folk, as accounts in popular literature have shown for hundreds of years. And the Feast of the Assumption has been in the Church's calendar since the Middle Ages. What is new is the proclamation in November 1950 of the Assumption as an infallible dogma and article of faith by the Pope. To Protestants and Rationalists this was a retrograde step, offending against the refined liberal-scientific prejudices of the age. But, as Jung said, the Pope was responding in the only way he could to an enormous popular demand for femininity to take its place in heaven and to become part of what is divine. The centuries of emphasis on the masculine God represented a disturbance in the balance between masculine and feminine which is the structure of the human psyche. The dogma of the Assumption restores the balance. This has a profound practical effect, for, in this final phase of the Christian aeon when man lives under the threat of a universal destruction of his own making, the emergence of the feminine, tender, merciful archetype may turn out to be one of our most hopeful signs: a sign of man's inner integration, of his learning to harmonise together the different aspects of his personality. And the image of the Virgin enthroned may become the most positively prophetic symbol of our time.

Finally, there is the need to show how all these eternal and pictorial images of the anima actually reflect themselves in the everyday life of the ordinary embodied man as he makes the journey through life from childhood to old age. It is time to look at the practical psychological events which are in every man the day-by-day working-out of all this symbolism in common experience. What follows is a sort of brief psychological biography.

From an early age men and boys are likely to reject the feminine side of their nature. We see examples in the school playground: the odium attracted by any boy who goes in for playing with dolls or for following some of life's gentler callings such as art, music and poetry. He will be called 'pansy', or worse. And then throughout life there is a widespread tendency to despise homosexuals: the derogatory jargon used to describe them and the cruel jokes often made at their expense is as much evidence as we need. But what is hatred of homosexuals except a projected fear of the reality of our own femininity?

In our youth it is good, if rather painful at times, to have many love-affairs – that is to encounter and integrate the anima-archetype of the Temptress or Enchantress. She is a part of man's personality, the woman within; and, if she is not met and integrated at the time of our youth, she will only emerge neurotically later on in the well-known and sorry figure of the middle-aged man in constant pursuit of young mistresses. He is having to catch up on a phase that was missed earlier in his life. The young mistresses may be real enough in the flesh and blood, but the function they perform is as the girls of his dreams. That unhappy, unbalanced forty-five-year-old has at last caught sight of his anima in her most lurid and sexually potent guise. The anima is unconscious. We fall into unconsciousness. The other expression is of 'falling in love'. Language always tells a story. And not just for forty-year-olds. Jung writes, 'When a respectable sep-tuagenarian runs off with a seventeen-year-old from the chorus line, we know that the gods have claimed another victim.'

The anima represents the emotional, feeling, intuitive aspects of a man's personality. So the man who has not integrated his anima is likely to be over-controlled, insisting on the utter sovereignty of logic and the need for a rational explanation for everything. He may be over-intellectual, calculating, mean. He is not likely to have much patience with his flighty teenage daughters: their excessive feminine behaviour will be only a threat to his exquisitely guarded masculinity. He has so much to deny in himself, so much to shut out and disown. Hope may come to him through an understanding wife who will personify her husband's anima. And if he can form a constructive, self-giving relationship with his wife, that may be the way towards his own integration. Or, risking moral censure, he may find a mistress – someone near his own age who will be his soulmate and companion, the one in whom he can come to see his own inwardness reflected.

The man who has integrated consciousness with the unconscious anima will be more relaxed, gentler, more secure without having to flex his macho muscles all the while. He will have that sense of balance and perspective that finds its best and most human expression in a sense of humour. It has been remarked already that a sense of humour is a sense of perspective dancing. Integration of consciousness and anima is true balance, true perspective: so humour, the ability to laugh at oneself, is the mark of the mature and integrated man.

Similarly, the anima or unconscious aspect, like sleep, is closely associated with death. The integrated man who has his masculine and feminine aspects in balance will not fear death. His anima, his soul, is not destroyed by death – which was the old religious way of expressing that eternal truth.

Not only the Christian Church, then, but every man, has everything to gain by the sincere attempt to integrate masculine and feminine aspects. To do less is to fall into spiritual and psychological imbalance which always has had consequences for institutions and individuals alike. More open and honest reflection is needed: a willingness to look inward at ourselves and, when we do not always like what we see, still steadfastly to refuse simply to project our dislikes on to others, be they women priests, homosexuals or folk we are quick to accuse of sexual impropriety.

As even the rumbustious God of the Old Testament at last discovered, the choice is to remain in the cold, arid desert or to find the true consort, Sophia, the tender intuitive wisdom of maturity and integration, the soulmate, the anima and the woman-within.

* * *

The sexual imagery in religion has been shaken to its depths by the ordination of women. This is not to say that women's ordination is a bad thing but only that such a sudden and radical innovation is bound to have profound psychological consequences.

Much has been written and said about the matter and not all of it, from supporters or opponents, has been edifying; but there is one aspect of the issue which I have nowhere heard discussed: the overtly sexual and erotic character of priesthood. Attention will inevitably be drawn now to this aspect because of the very visible differences between male and female priests.

'Priestcraft' is the word which acquired a distasteful connotation at the time of the Reformation, a connotation from which it has never escaped. The priest – and so the woman priest – does have a craft nonetheless. And it is a mistake to imagine that Christian priesthood is entirely separate and pure, free from the disturbing sexual currents which run deep in all forms of sacrificial religion – deeper by far than the tradition for young spinsters of the parish to go all dewy-eyed over the curate.

The reason why there have been such powerful emotions stirred by the argument over women's ordination is precisely sexual and erotic. The priest is an ambiguous figure who represents God to the people in blessing and absolution, and the people to God in supplication and in the offering of the sacrifice which is the Eucharist or the Holy Communion.

This is the crux. The priest may also be the cheerful, bumbling country vicar who stands up in the middle of Matins to announce the date and time of the next whist drive or the choir trip, but he is also the handler and mediator of sacred objects and mysteries. That is what all the emotion was about in the debate about women's ordination. No one, after all, would have been exercised or incensed about whether a woman might perform non-sacramental acts in church – making announcements, reading, preaching and so on. These things have been done for years.

But when even the humblest country vicar puts on the priest's vestments and enters the sanctuary, he becomes a mystical, mythological figure enacting timeless spiritual (i.e. psychological) processes. Or else why bother with vestments, sanctuary and ritual?

To represent what is eternal in the flux of time, the priest requires mystical symbols and a poetic, paradoxical language. These things are provided in the liturgy which is not just a form of words for a committee-meeting but the script for a divine-human drama.

The priest – and so the woman priest – carries the sins of the people to the altar and through the words of the sacrifice these are expiated. In primitive societies this was no mere metaphor or symbolic act, for often it was the priest himself who was sacrificed. In ancient Israel, from where the Christian notion of priesthood was derived, the priest-king was ritually and symbolically killed in order to fructify the earth.

It is not difficult to see how these two aspects – sin and fertility – are closely connected and intensely sexual. They are basic to life itself. In some tribes the fructifying was both symbolic and actual with the discharge of priestly semen at the climax of the ecstatic ritual. And ecstasy, whether regarded as religious or secular, is in fact one and indivisible.

This fact is proved by the language of sacrifice and anyone who doubts it has only to turn to the poems of

'ecstatic union' by St John of the Cross and a hundred
other mystics: these contain language which is explicitly
sexual, all about 'piercing', being 'ravished' and 'filled',
'transported' and so on. Mystic communion and sexual
union are part of the same reality.

This is obviously dangerous. That is precisely why
we have developed a priesthood. In the highly moral
liturgy of the Christian Church, sin and fructification,
sacrifice and death, are accommodated within a heavenly, ethical story of atonement. And it is the priest's
'craft' to represent this in the symbols and drama of
liturgy.

Every time there is a service of Holy Communion, the
cosmic Christ, like the ancient priest-king, dies and rises
again to take the community of the faithful people to
wife: the Bible describes the Church as the Bride of
Christ.

When the priest represents the person of Christ in the
giving of his body in both the sacrifice for sin and in the
heavenly marriage – 'which is the union betwixt Christ
and his Church' – the overtly sexual character of the
drama is mitigated by certain protective symbols. The
priest is distanced from physical touch by going into the
sanctuary on his own. The body and blood are not
corporeal but sacramental – bread and wine – and they
are discreetly veiled. The explicit masculinity is dis-
guised under the appearance of feminine (even
effeminate) vestments and lace.

But the phallic and ecstatic elements remain, as they
must in the candles, in the incense, in the words 'This is
my body' and in the mythology of eating and drinking
the flesh and blood of the Bridegroom who is Christ
represented by the priest. This is no extreme outlandish
interpretation; it is all there in the words of the service

book used in thousands of English churches every Sunday morning – even in the *Alternative Service Book* (1980).

The liturgy as it now stands is something developed over 2000 years – and with its origins far back in the primeval consciousness – to enable the Church to accommodate satisfactorily the ever-present realities of Eros and Thanatos (sex and death) and to do so in a way which removes guilt and promotes social cohesiveness. Not even the modern services with their democratic inventions have altered the essence of this ritual, spiritual communion and psychodrama.

This ritual, what now goes on in churches throughout the land, is something that has evolved slowly and painfully. The ordination of women, by its nature, could not be a gradual development. It happened suddenly: on the morning of 12 March 1994 there were at least a dozen legally ordained women priests in Bristol.

This is necessarily a radical, revolutionary change. I do not say that therefore it should not have happened. But for God's sake let us reflect on the nature and consequences for the human psyche of what we are doing. The ordination of women will have political and social consequences. These have been examined and mulled over in great detail. There will also be profound psychological consequences. These have not been seriously considered.

How shall we cope with the excess of feminine symbolism in the sanctuary? What will be the emotional, sexual, erotic and spiritual results of our hearing a soprano or contralto voice speak the words of the masculine Christ: 'This is my body'? Or long blonde hair overhanging a gorgeous chasuble?

What when, in celebrations of the Holy Commu-

nion where the woman priest faces the congregation
– as is now the general practice – the lineaments of
the female form are discerned representing the masculine Saviour? Or what of the paradox of a woman
as the Bridegroom? How does the Church become the
Bride of Christ when the figure who represents Christ
is a woman?

Now that we have women priests, it is vital that we
examine carefully these issues of practical psychology.
In fact their discussion ought to have been part all along
of the debate about women's ordination.

Religion is meant to bind and to unify, to make our
divided selves whole: that is what salvation means. If,
confident that we have appraised all the political and
social issues arising out of women's ordination, we now
blunder ahead unprepared, uncomprehending of the
psychological factors, we may find that, instead of a
wholeness, we have inflicted upon ourselves a terrify-
ing confusion and dissociation.

Everything which I have written in this chapter is from
a man's point of view: given my sex, this cannot be
helped. But there is another reason for the masculine
bias and this too cannot be avoided.

Western culture and civilisation has very largely
been written up from the man's point of view. The
feminists are right when they say that we have lived in
a paternalistic society for three thousand years or more.
No doubt in some ways this has been a very bad thing
and we may deplore this tendency in western culture;
but we are not at liberty to deny what has happened. As
a matter of historical fact our literature, painting, music
and our social and political institutions have been masculine productions.

A male-dominated civilisation is our cultural story and so, for better and for worse, our psychology and spirituality has been constructed and perpetuated by 'the man's point of view'. This may be unfortunate. The whole epoch may have been a ghastly mistake. But we cannot help it; we cannot avoid or deny historical facts without, in the process, doing violence to the truth about the past and so necessarily misperceiving present realities.

Of course the old order is changing. The doctrine of the Assumption and the ordination of women have shifted the theological foundations and begun to move the church towards a greater and more constructive acknowledgement of femininity. In the secular world, women's role in western society has altered beyond recognition in a generation.

In his influential book *The Uses of Literacy* (1957), Richard Hoggart described married women aged only twenty-nine as shapeless lumps who moved only between the kitchen and the ironing board. Forty years later, women hold high positions in industry, commerce and the professions and Britain has appointed (and dismissed!) its first woman Prime Minister. No longer shapeless lumps, under the influence of glossy television series, women can now be sirens at sixty.

Why and how have these fundamental changes come about so rapidly? There are many economic, sociological and psychological causes to account for the swift transformation in the role of women but most significant of them all is the development of instant communications through the electronic media.

This is the single development which has made possible all the radical changes in modern society. Movements are accelerated by the flow of ideas, words and images and it is these things which the electronic media are able to transmit with the greatest facility. In the electronic age everything moves faster and this is bound to be true also of cultural change.

The culture, in its secular and religious aspects, is already being re-read and reinterpreted in the light of the feminist advances and we live in swift, heady times as event and interpretation chase each other in the frenetic dance of electronic communications.

A cultural phenomenon now arises, dominates and declines in a very short time. Stars rise and fall in a season. Our motto might be 'Famous for fifteen minutes'. This makes interpretation and assessment extraordinarily difficult because there is so little time in which to consider and evaluate a phenomenon before it disappears only to be replaced with another. It becomes much more difficult in such an age to distinguish between what is truly radical, innovative and of lasting importance and what is ephemeral, a nine days' wonder and a mere flash in the pan.

This uncomfortable fact does not relieve us of the responsibility for trying to make sense of our age; but we are living with new and perplexing difficulties and the demands of our own technological invention.

It is plain, however, that the redressing of the cultural balance in favour of women is a process that is gathering pace and energy. As with every other cultural development there will be advantages and disadvantages, but it is as yet too early to see clearly the full extent of these great changes.

Western culture is living through the psychological equivalent of an earthquake. But already the story of the upheaval is being told. The task, which will be both the test of our psychological and spiritual wholeness and the key to our future well-being, is to relate the new story to the old one without a disjunction in plot so violent that it destroys our credibility as a civilisation.

7

What Should We Teach the Children?

When the teacher asked her class of juniors to draw the flight into Egypt, one little boy drew an aeroplane with a very dashing figure in the cockpit. 'And who's that?' the teacher asked.

'That's Pontius the Pilate!'

Any Religious Education teacher has a huge stock of howlers. These are humorous linguistic accidents which arise out of the subject's difficulty. Teaching religion must involve teaching the Bible and this inevitably makes for confusion. The child wants to know whether the Bible stories are true, or what is the difference between them and tales of ancient Greece or Fairy stories. Fairly soon, then, the question of the authority of the Bible arises.

There are three main attitudes towards this authority. First, the strictly literal and fundamentalist approach. 'The Bible says . . .' so it must be true. This attitude is less widespread these days when syllabuses have to be agreed – even in Church Schools – with the Local Education Department. This rather fierce and uncompromising approach has generally tended to do more harm than good, since, as soon as the teacher's authority over the pupil is removed, the pupil is likely to rebel against religion entirely – 'That load of old rubbish that Miss Whatsername used to give us!' The fundamentalist approach is even more anachronistic these days when science is taught from an early age.

Secondly, there is the attitude expressed: 'This is what some people believe. You're free to make up your own mind.' And this is often augmented by readings from the scriptures of other world-religions, and with brief accounts of the origins and heroes of those religions. It is like a sort of Supermarket of Faith: a bit of this and a bit of that; a bit of what you fancy does you good. 'St Paul believed this, Mahomet believed that and Guatama believed the other. What d'you believe, Sharon?'

It is all decently and liberally done, from the best motives, but it is not teaching religion. It is teaching secularism and relativism because it assumes there is a neutral point from which one can have a perspective on all religions. There is such a point, of course, but it cannot be a religious point, because religion is about what is most true and binding: it is about authority and commitment. You cannot be committed to a collage of religious excerpts.

Nevertheless, there must be some sympathy for the teacher who tries to teach in this way. What else, in a free society, is he supposed to do? There is an ethical dislike of 'indoctrination'.

I believe there is a third way, but it involves the necessity of coming off the fence and making up our minds on an important issue: do we accept that the

Christian Faith has *authority* in this land? (We need not define that authority too rigidly at the outset.) Or are we a secular, scientific culture with the same sort of interest in religion as the archaeologist has in old pots? The attitude towards religion which may be summarised as 'This is what people used to believe in the funny old days' is both patronising and useless. There is something distastefully arrogant in the assumption that, 'Of course, we know better than the ancients.' Besides, it is not self-evidently clear that we do know better.

Let us try to dispel suspicions about so-called 'indoctrination' by noticing that the secular, scientific attitude to religion is itself a doctrine and there is no reason why that point of view should be accepted as true rather than, say, one of the world-religions at which it casts its omniscient glances. The assumption of secularism is itself a prejudice.

'Make up your own mind' sounds to be a good liberal maxim. But minds need to be made up of something. A child or young person cannot make judgements in a vacuum. He has to be informed first. To take examples from nonreligious areas of the curriculum: the Whig view of history is taught as if it were axiomatic – whereas there is, to say the least, some doubt about this. We teach Euclidean geometry and give not a fig for doubts, but the logical innovations by men such as Frege, Tarski and Bertrand Russell have rendered it, in some respects, quite obsolete. Rightly, we do not expect the child to be instantly versed in higher historical criticism or the propositional calculus before he can be said to know anything about history or maths. Learning is a process of induction and introduction. We begin at the beginning: '1 + 1 = 2'; 'In 1066, William won the Battle of Hastings'; 'Now the birth of Jesus Christ was thus. . . .' Criticism cannot precede understanding. How could it? It would mean that you were criticising what you did not comprehend. Unfortunately, that is no bar to some people.

We must look at the way in which learning actually proceeds. It is by means of practice and familiarisation – of getting to know, in fact. The man who knows his subject thoroughly is like a swimmer at home in the water. And, of course, it is the knowledgeable person – and not the ignoramus – who is the best critic. Sharon cannot judge a subject until she knows what the subject is about. This is why the injunction to 'make up your own mind' can so often be spurious, seeming-intelligent and yet hypocritical. How can a child who is unable to recite the Creed, the Lord's Prayer and the Ten Commandments 'Make up his mind' on the issue of whether Buddha or Mahomet is closer to God?

Open-mindedness and the broad approach can extend to absurd lengths. There is the Local Authority's Agreed Syllabus for Upper Juniors in Sunderland, for instance, where nine-year-olds are prescribed 'the Life of Krishna, Indus Valley civilisation, life and customs of India, some notion of reincarnation and the role of Brahmins'. I hope all this is not expected to be achieved before afternoon playtime! Notice that they are to learn about *reincarnation*. There are some 'specialists' who would regard learning about the *Incarnation* of Christ as indoctrination! Muhammad and Buddha are on the schedule too. In Muhammad's case, the pupil is asked to pay special attention to the prophet's attack on polytheism, and in the case of Buddha, he must study his previous lives and enlightenment.

No one is enlightened by this sort of thing. I have suffered the difficult task of trying to make the multicultural syllabus work and I know what the children's first question is: 'Is Lord Krishna a Lord like Lord Jesus?' The insistence that children should attend to all these things goes oddly with the assumption that the Incarnation and the Resurrection of Christ are 'too difficult'. The idea of providing a sort of overview of all religions – along with that unspoken assumption 'We know better now, of course' – is an arrogant idea. It amounts to brainwashing with liberal values.

Let us come back to first principles – not specifically about Religious Education, but about teaching and learning in general. What does it mean to have learnt something? It may seem a silly question, but what answer we give is bound to influence our whole aim and idea of education. Suppose I answer a silly question with an equally silly reply: 'To have learnt something means that you know it.' And to know something is to have it available, in your head – or, as we used to say, 'by heart'. The mechanistic, behaviouristic age has invaded the classroom too: now they say not 'by heart' but 'by rote' – as a way of despising formal learning.

I must labour the point: either you know something or you do not know it. In order to know something, you must learn it. The easiest way of learning is to be taught. So, to return, what should we teach?

Forget the Orwellian overtones, there must be some indoctrination. This means simply the putting-in of doctrines. It does not necessarily involve coercion and brainwashing. Why have we left to us only the negative connotations of the word 'indoctrination'? Perhaps it is because we are dominated by a liberal dictatorship which teaches that the only virtue in education and learning is the conjuror's ability to hold *all* opinions simultaneously – contradictions notwithstanding?

Minds have to be filled with something. Sharon cannot 'make up her own mind' unless she has been given something of substance on which her mind can work. How can she arbitrate between the great religious cultures of the world on a smattering from the new glossy textbook? The idea is ridiculous. A Muslim boy learns the *Koran* off by heart. Years and years it takes him.

To pay less attention to religion than that – and yet to claim to know one's mind on the subject – is an absurdity. Take our Sharon again: what if, instead of giving her the smattering, we teach her the faith, induct and initiate her into it over the years? Then she may end up devout, or she may conclude herself an atheist. At least she will have been given something substantial – something on which she can reasonably, informedly, 'make up her mind'.

But this is indoctrination, say the liberals. They mean it is making someone believe something against his will. This is not the way education and learning works. The informed person is not the one who is gullible, at the mercy of every would-be dictator and psychological-political manipulator. It is the ignorant person who is captive to all sorts of nonsense in the way of ideas and doctrines. Moreover, it is the informed person who makes the most radical criticisms of that about which he has been informed. What could Einstein have said by way of amending Newton if he had not first known the works of Newton inside out? How could Freud have invented the creative psychoanalytic concept of the Oedipus Complex if he had never read Sophocles? Jesus could never have superseded the Old Testament if he had not known the Old Testament intimately. In other words, we have nothing to fear from initiation into a tradition. Tradition does not bind expression: it liberates it. The only people who are unliberated are those unfortunate enough to have remained in ignorance. To understand a tradition is to be in a position to criticise it. Ask Leavis and Eliot, Schoenberg and Van Gogh – traditionalists, all of them, 'brainwashed' and 'indoctrinated' into a particular way of seeing; all of them producing the most original and critical works imaginable.

Tradition and originality are not opposites but necessary complements.

Is a batsman who has learned how to play his strokes more or less free when he faces the fast bowler than the batsman who has never practised but trusts to luck and inspiration? Why do all the great pianists practise for hours each day? Does the constant repetition of practice inhibit them and spoil their playing? Are they 'indoctrinated' by it? Is a lawyer who knows the law a worse advocate than one who does not know it? These questions answer themselves. So why should it be imagined that things work differently in the matter of religion?

It is tiresome to have to labour the point like this, but it is necessary because all the 'educational theory' runs in the opposite direction. Things have become so muddled in contemporary thought that it is a duty at times to state the obvious lest it should come to seem less than obvious. That this muddle is, as it were, imposed by 'liberals' and 'progressives' who hold all the best seats is regrettable and perhaps even the touchstone for a polemical blast: but, short of making the point, I want to spend little time in polemics and more in making practical suggestions – now that a certain amount of dust has been cleared.

It is nonsense to say that anyone is harmed by being introduced to a valid tradition. If by some an introduction should be called indoctrination, then by all means let us have more indoctrination. The tradition which is ours stretches back into the ancient Middle-Eastern culture and civilisations of Egypt and Phoenicia, and, particularly as expressed in the Old Testament, the monotheistic insights of the Jews. Alongside these things are also to be found Greek myths, legends and philosophy. There are the Fathers of the Early Church, Medieval Philosophy and Theology as taught by Anselm and Aquinas; the Reformation and Counter Reformation; the Renaissance; Kant; Shakespeare; Bach; Luther. And then the modern period: George Eliot; Freud; Schoenberg; Karl Barth; T. S. Eliot. The eminent moderns are no less modern for their being traditionalists. Two books especially illustrate this – books by the most revolutionary traditionalist of our century, T. S. Eliot – *The Idea of a Christian Society* and *Tradition and the Individual Talent*.

This is the tradition that we should teach, hand on and live out in our lives. Not all before lunch, of course, as they do with comparative religion in the Sunderland Agreed Syllabus – and in many other places. So where do we begin?

Religious Education should begin at the mother's knee and at infant school with Bible stories. They should be read out of the *Authorised Version of the Bible*. It is above all strange that a generation which prides itself on 'universal literacy' should claim that these versions of the stories are beyond the reach of children, that children cannot understand them. This is a gross insult to 300 years of children who had no other Bible except the *Authorised Version* but who were not thought to be so stupid that *they* could not understand what was being read to them.

Of course, we know what is meant by the claim that the *Authorised Version* is beyond young children: it is the fashionable claim that it is 'elitist' and 'irrelevant', that it does not 'fit into the child's experience'. Well, it surely does not if the child's experience is the vacuous chat and raucous din of many children's television programmes – studio games, pop, grunt-and-gargle language in which all the presenters have mid-Atlantic accents and the subject matter is pop stars, money and noise.

By contrast, the words of the *Authorised Version* have shaped English *oral* and *literary* culture for nearly 400 years. It is impossible to understand the great poets and novelists of our tradition unless you know something of the Bible. More than that, ordinary speech, even in the 1990s, is saturated with biblical phrases employed in both biblical and non-biblical contexts. I will give a few examples at random. For good measure, some of these examples will be from the *Book of Common Prayer* (1662). So intertwined are these sources of our common language that only an expert or extreme pedant will know which are from the Bible and which from the Prayer Book: 'Be fruitful and multiply'; 'The tree of Knowledge'; 'Flesh of my flesh'; 'Unto dust thou shalt return'; 'My brother's keeper'; 'The mark of Cain'; 'A pillar of salt'; 'Mess of potage'; 'Corn in Egypt'; 'Coat of many colours'; 'Stranger in a strange land'; 'A land flowing with milk and honey'; 'Burning bush', 'Eye for eye and tooth for tooth'; 'Scapegoat'; 'The everlasting arms'; 'Hip and thigh'; 'Quit yourselves like men'; 'God Save the King'; 'A man after his own heart'; 'Played the fool'; 'Passing the love of women'; 'A still small voice'; 'Painted her face'; 'Job's comforters'; 'I know that my Redeemer liveth'; 'Hope deferred'; 'Spare the rod'; 'Pride before a fall'; 'Coals of Fire'; 'Vanity of vanities';

'A time to be born and a time to die'; 'One man in a thousand'; 'Cast thy bread upon the waters'; 'Rose of Sharon'; 'Woe is me'; 'Watchman, what of the night?'

And this is only a smattering. To deprive a child of this legacy is to cut him off from the living tradition of Western civilisation which is an endless fund of quotation and cross-reference, every phrase and sentence that is right illuminating every other. To offer some new translation instead is . . . well, to sell the birthright for a mess of potage.

'Minds must be made up of something.' What we put in when we teach *determines* the shape and quality of the mind. As the Bible itself says:

'Train up a child in the way he should go; and when he is old, he will not depart from it.'

(Proverbs 22:6)

But, it is objected, the *Authorised Version* is difficult. It is not more difficult than much modern literature and modern translations of the Bible. But in any case, everything is fairly difficult to begin with – as I was forever saying to the congregation when they claimed not to know a hymn I had chosen on a Sunday morning: 'You didn't know *Onward Christian Soldiers* once!'

The best method is always to give the best. And the best translation of the Bible into English, the *Authorised Version*, does not give the child who is taught it *only* the Bible: it sets up connections with all subsequent writings in English. It introduces him to an oral collection of phrase and fable, nuance, quote and reference that amounts to nothing less than a history and practice of English language – and *therefore* of thought – over the last half-millennium.

There is no reason to be afraid of the *Authorised*

Version. It is actually written in a much more basic, Anglo-Saxon style than much modern prose: it is certainly a lot easier to understand than communications from the Gas companies or Government circulars about the Citizens' Charter. It is plainly written, in a style that many of our contemporary fiction writers could learn from. The story of Joseph and the coat of many colours, of the destruction of Sodom and Gomorrah, Jacob's ladder, the parables of Jesus – they are all so sparely and brilliantly told: no rush of adjectives to add 'colour'; no 'padding' or striving after effect, but a directness that is so strong and evocative it is never forgotten. 'A certain man went down from Jerusalem to Jericho and fell among thieves . . .' Or, 'And they crucified him there.' No purple passages. The *Authorised Version* refreshes parts of our literary sensitivities and awareness that other books cannot reach.

I was not introduced to it in any intellectual sense. It was just my grandma's black Bible which happened to be lying around in the back bedroom. I began at the beginning. Magic. 'The voice of God walking in the garden in the cool of the evening.' Abraham. Isaac, Jacob. Joseph. Moses and the burning bush. Then, I will admit, it gets boring for a six-year-old: all those rules and regulations in *Leviticus*. But it perks up again when Elijah with his chariot of fire appears, and when Daniel tells about the burning fiery furnace and Belshazzar's Feast. (Did somebody say, 'The writing's on the wall'?)

These stories and, of course, the stories of Jesus should be read to the young who may then be encouraged to talk about them, draw pictures, act them out in little classroom dramas, tell the stories in their own words, and so on. So the stories that are the bedrock of our life and literature are truly imbibed like mother's milk – read, marked, learned and inwardly digested. To the accusations of 'elitism' and 'irrelevance' I would say simply that to offer them less than the best is to deprive them.

The question of whether the stories are true or not should not be met head on when dealing with our youngest pupils. For the issue of truth – while it may sound simple enough – is, in reality, very elusive. We know that the stories are true in that they have shaped our language and the language of our best writers so that we cannot ever escape their power. But the scientific outlook and prejudice has made every question about truth into an empirical question: Did it happen just as it says? I have found that, if you teach the Bible stories decently and reverently, the question of empirical truth (limited as it is, in any case) will arise, but it will not much matter. Sharon and Jeremy in Class Three will ask if the story – of Jacob's Ladder, say – is true. The thing to do is to throw it back at them: What do you think? They will nearly always say something thoughtful and sensible: 'It could have been just a dream.'

Indeed it could. And where is the loss in that? Talking about the stories with young children does not undermine the authority of the stories but, rather, increases their power and influence. We should not patronise and underrate young children: they often know that stories are not true, perhaps, in the way that $2 + 2 = 4$ is true; but they recognise that the stories are not therefore meaningless or plain false. A story is a story. And children know in a rudimentary sense what the good critic of a novel knows: it is not a question of empirical truth – 'Did it actually happen, just like that?' – but whether the tale rings true. The child knows intuitively that the story which rings true *is* true. 'A certain man went down from Jerusalem to Jericho and fell among thieves' – is that true, or was it a story made up by Jesus? The point is this: The parable of the Good Samaritan is just as true whether Jesus remembered it or whether he invented it. And it is almost certain that he invented it. The Divine fiction is better, more compelling, than mere empiricism.

The Bible stories have created half of Western civilisation. The other half is based on the Greek myths and philosophy. One half of this civilisation is the Christian Church, and in the Church the Bible stories are set within the framework of an annual cycle. Even in modern, secular times, this still provides the temporal landmarks: Christmas, Easter, Whitsuntide – maddening as it is for a traditional believer to find himself in a world where Whitsun has become Spring Bank Holiday and Halloween is all that All Saints is remembered for. Still, the framework remains and so it may as well be used.

It can be done to great effect. Last year our local junior school produced the most evocative Nativity Play that I have seen in a quarter of a century's close association as teacher or parson with all kinds of schools. This play used only the words of the *Authorised Version*'s Gospel accounts. So, for instance, we carried no extra baggage such as 'the innkeeper' who usually appears – and who therefore has to have lines composed for him – although he does not appear in the biblical text. Following the Bible's words has the merit of actually taking less effort than writing your own. They are words which can be trusted. The effect even on a suburban audience – fairly secular, fairly philistine; Dad came along with his flash camera to click away at the 'angel' Victoria – was spellbinding.

Then there is Easter. I used to teach in a downtown secondary school in industrial Lancashire and I was fairly well into gimmicks in taking assemblies. You had to find some way of subverting the little (and not so little) darlings' more antisocial eruptions. Faithfully, I did what the modern schoolteacher is expected to do and rooted most of my teaching in pop music and television. The response was lukewarm to say the least. One Easter, for Holy Week assemblies, I simply read the account of Our Lord's Last Supper, Gethsemane, arrest, trial and crucifixion. Bare as that. With traditional hymns: *There is a Green Hill* and *When I Survey*. To my astonishment, the hall was silently attentive, alive with something close to reverence.

There are the weekly Collects from the *Book of Common Prayer*. These are beautiful and succinct, the very model of what prayer should be. They are rhythmical and they all follow the same form. They can usefully be learned by heart. 'Minds must be filled with something.' Young minds filled with twenty or thirty of the Prayer Book Collects are not minds that have been deprived. They are the basis of a whole way of thinking. They are the best introduction to the study of English that I know. Youngsters will love to copy them out and learn them, write them in a special notebook, write their own prayers on the opposite page, pretend they are monks with their illuminated manuscripts. It works better than the supermarket of faiths, and, once again, it has the merit that most of the work is done for the teacher in the form of the texts: certainly anything he himself invents is not likely to surpass the Collects for beauty and clarity of expression. Besides, these Collects define true religion. They have deep understanding into human psychology. This makes them the perfect introduction not to 'beautiful language', but to true and accurate thinking. Nobody was ever made worse by being given something better.

The same might be said of that old thing, the catechism, which children once again were required to learn 'by heart'. Of course, it all sounds very staid to your whizz-bang educationalists of today with their charts and graphs and computer printouts of 'systems of morality', 'ethical relativism' and the like. But actually the catechism is the logical next step in Religious Education, after the Bible stories. It contains the Creed, the Lord's Prayer and the Ten Commandments. Any English child at the age of twelve – the traditional age for Confirmation – who does not know these three short texts can barely be said to have become acquainted with religion at all.

The Creed introduces him to what the Church officially believes. It opens the gate to systematic theology. There is room enough for discussion and argument in the Apostles' Creed to keep class and teacher talking for ever.

The Lord's Prayer is the introduction to all prayer. It is remarkably comprehensive. It places the child in a worshipping tradition that goes back to New Testament times. The teacher might copy it out for them in Greek and Latin, so that the children can hear how amazingly similar the *rhythm* of that prayer has remained since the time of Jesus.

The Ten Commandments are the backbone of all morality and not just of Judaeo-Christian morality. They originate in Babylon, in the Code of Hammurabi which predates Moses by some centuries; and there is no moral code anywhere on earth even today that does not include most if not all of them. This is because they are *constitutive* of morality, of the logic of moral language: because it is not possible to form a moral code based on the *opposites* of these Commandments without destroying society itself. You could not legislate on the lines 'Kill!', 'Steal!', 'Commit Adultery!' So to introduce a child to the Ten Commandments is to introduce him to how the world – or most of it – thinks ethically. These Commandments also provide material for discussion and for the development of the child's own moral sense. To any who think this approach is rather staid and stuffy, I would say it is the centre of our spiritual, moral and intellectual history – what has made us what we are. And there are no boring subjects, only uninteresting (because uninterested) and incompetent teachers.

Religious Education is not complete without introducing the pupil to the great religious art works of the Christian era. We are fortunate that there are so many of them. We do not need to go immediately to the Vatican or Notre-Dame. The local parish church will do: its shape, its architecture, the vestments and furniture. The Hymnbook itself is an introduction to English poetry. The hymns of Wesley and Cowper are a spiritual heritage and object lesson by themselves. The tunes of Dykes are a first lesson in composition in that classical form, the four-line hymn.

With a thousand years of Christian painting and music from medieval plainchant to Benjamin Britten and beyond, the teaching of Religious Education can be an introduction to the best that the Western mind and its art has created. In every town and in most villages there is a church, and these are often the best buildings in the locality. There are graveyards – local history in stone. There are church registers, which can tell you more about the history of the local community than any other source. And then there are visits to the great cathedrals and abbeys.

Religious Education in this style is the way to unlock the past, but it is not just that fascinating, historical thing: for the past has made us what we are; the language and images of the church and its monumental presence in the community, in the landscape, continue to influence English life at the close of the second millennium.

It would be an act of foolish and doctrinaire neglect for anyone trusted with the education of children to turn aside from these tangible realities in favour of the supermarket of faiths or the patronising attitude, 'This is what people *used* to believe.' For it is a matter of fact that Christian art and culture, Christian philosophy and psychology – from St Augustine to Carl Gustav Jung – remain the single most fertile influence on everything that we are.

Recent statements on behalf of the government have reinforced what remains of the traditional concept of Britain as a Christian country. The government says rightly that the Christian faith should be the mainspring of religious education. It has been decided, then, that what should be taught are the elements of Christianity rather than 'multiculturalism' – the dogmatic secular liberalism which regards all religions and none as being of equal value.

There is nothing sectarian or exclusive about this policy which puts Christianity at the centre of religious education. There are opt-out clauses for those of other faiths who wish to have their children taught accordingly.

I discussed the teaching of religion with the Chief Rabbi, Dr Jonathan Sachs, as I was preparing this chapter. Dr Sachs said: 'You best acknowledge and tolerate another person's tradition when you are well-versed in your own tradition. The idea of religious freedom must involve the freedom to belong to a particular religion. And there is nothing to say that a firm commitment to your own way is incompatible with a profound respect for other ways.'

8

A National Church?

Unless otherwise informed, the British Army would always label its soldiers 'C. of E.' This practice was often sneered at by men who belonged to more exotic denominations and who knew that, though you might claim to be Church of England, you probably had not darkened the church porch since your Aunt Agnes' funeral more years ago than anyone could remember.

But the appellation of 'C. of E.', used as the army used it, made historical sense. The English Church was founded in the sixteenth century and there followed a hundred and fifty years of schism and civil war – in which, in 1649, a King of England went to the scaffold. The Church that was hammered out of all this strife and contention was the Church of the King James Bible and the Book of Common Prayer. It was intended, as Hooker said, to be a church for all the people: 'Every man of England a member of the Church of England.' It was for the idle and the perplexed, the wicked and the curmudgeonly as well as for the great and the good, the virtuous and the devout.

At bottom, it was a political settlement of genius. It accommodated all sorts and conditions of men without stringent religious tests. It was a bastion against the kind of 'enthusiasm' and opportunism that were dangerous in themselves, that had led to schisms and civil war. It played into the hands of neither Rome nor the extreme Reformers – Calvinists, Zwinglians, Anabaptists and so on. It was a settlement which gave us a decent set of political liberties in this country for 300 years. What did it demand? That you should honour the Monarch and make your Communion three times in the year, of which Easter should be one. It abolished the authority of foreign prelates, especially the Popes of Rome, who were not, in the sixteenth and seventeenth centuries, such benign religious devotees as the present occupant of that seat. 'The Pope of Rome hath no jurisdiction in this realm of England.' Also, by setting the King as the Church's Head and ordering a system of ecclesiastical hierarchy and Church courts which were always legally and politically related closely to secular authorities, it created a national polity which delivered us from the opposite extreme to Rome: individual men as laws unto themselves, interpreting the Bible as they themselves chose, bounden to no jurisdiction but their own opinions – dressed up though these might be in a devotional language borrowed from such as Luther. In other words, the Anglican Settlement was a middle way between tyranny and anarchy. It was a National Church.

It has stood us well these last few centuries, giving to all Englishmen a spiritual, as well as a temporal, home and rites of passage: Baptism, Matrimony and a decent Burial without strict religious tests. The Anglican

Settlement was further improved and strengthened by genuinely liberal Acts for the toleration of Roman Catholics and Dissenters – particularly the Repeal of the Test Act in 1828 and the Catholic Emancipation Act of 1829 and other Acts to open the universities to Dissenters. Final authority is vested in Parliament and not in the bishops. This is very important because it means that the Church of England is truly a Church for all the people and not a sect for the committed and like-minded; for those who find whatever ecclesiastical hierarchy may be in office amenable.

Looking at the history of the English Church these thirty years, I cannot escape the conclusion that it has shot itself in the foot. Either because they do not understand the concept of a National Church, or because they wish to ascribe power to themselves, the recent and present hierarchies are doing their best to get authority back from Parliament and into the hands of professional churchmen – that is, the bishops and the new bureaucracy, the General Synod.

So instead of its being the spiritual aspect of the realm, the Church of England has set itself apart from the polity in which it lives. It has invented its own prayers in the form of the Alternative Service Book. In this book, the bishops have put themselves above the Queen in the intercessions at the Holy Communion. Doctrine and practice are being taken out of the hands of Parliament and made a matter for the professional clergy and the Synod. The Synod has even become known as 'the Church's Parliament'. This is a deceit: we have one Parliament in this realm of England and it meets at Her Majesty's behest in the House of Commons and the House of Lords. Contemporary bishops and synodsmen think they know better than that which can be expressed as the mind of the body politic. So they have turned the National Church into a sect. Well, they have not entirely succeeded. After all, a few hundred years of religious practice and precedent is not undone in five minutes. The *Book of Common Prayer* – though rarely used – is still the official Prayer Book and standard of doctrine for the Church. The Queen is still its Head. Some parsons still have freehold rights over their vicarages and this means that they have rights of ownership in law and so they cannot be fired just because the local diocesan bishop is not fond of them. Some livings are still in the hands of private patrons – landowners, industrialists, corporations and so on.

This is very vexatious to some 'progressive' clergy and layfolk. They despise the Anglican Settlement as out of date, 'Erastian' and obscure; but chiefly they hate the arrangement so finely wrought because it sets a limit to their personal power. 'Why,' they argue, 'shouldn't *we* make the decisions? We are, after all, the ones who have been trained in theological matters. We are the experts.'

The quality of the training and the expertise may, on the record of recent pronouncements and publications, be a cause for some disquiet. But, in any case, the Church of England was never meant to be run by trained experts. It was meant to be a spiritual and political home for all Englishmen. Trained experts get carried away on the backs of their own expertise: they become enthusiasts of one sort or another: Puritans and Levellers, doctrinaire Protestants, Extemporists, Methodists – in short, they become sectarians with more regard for their private fancies than for the public as a whole, as a Commonwealth. (See the preface to the *Book of Common Prayer* on this issue.)

In my opinion, the destruction of the Anglican Settlement – if not by decree then by a gradual chipping away at its foundations, which has been the main preoccupation of Synod – is a bad thing. For it means that the Church is no longer a dimension of the realm – the spiritual aspect of the realm – but merely a party within the State. People ask these days whether you are a Christian. Fifty years ago the question would not have arisen. It was assumed that you were a Christian unless you declared yourself opted out. You were, as it said at the bottom of the Private Soldier's bed in the hospital wing, 'C. of E.' Nowadays, you do not opt out. You opt in. This is right against the spirit of Anglicanism, which was always inclusive. It divides people into 'committed' and 'uncommitted'. It has made an open society into a private club. Is it really as bad as I am making out? Yes, because, for instance, the Synod is talking about tests before a child is baptised, before a couple may be married in church. They want to be able to ask about the degree of commitment with which parents and engaged couples approach these ministrations. This is a narrowing, a tourniquet on the free circulation of traditional Anglicanism, which always declared that a man's religious commitment is a matter for himself, his conscience and the Lord God. Of course, the parson – all parsons – would rather that everyone came to church every week, that their commitment was excellent: but we have no right to demand it. The Church is not a holy club. And the Sacraments are not meant to be received only at the end of an obstacle race.

The dangers of sectarianism are increased by the inescapable fact that a sect or party is always likely to be dominated and controlled by like-minded men. There was always a measure of truth in this, even when the Anglican Settlement was going strong: it was satirised as 'The Tory Party at Prayer'. At least, it could never have been that officially, for its own political apparatus precluded the identification. Now that the Establishment ties are much looser – and some would have them abolished altogether – the Church of England looks much more like 'The Labour Party at the Barricades', or at least 'The Liberals at the Sherry Party'.

This is a pity for, while no doubt most political parties have something to offer to the public good and the ordering of our national life, no one party should be exclusively identified with Christian principles. But this is what has happened. In issue after issue, debate after synodical debate, the 'Christian Position' on everything from South Africa to the inner cities is equated with that of the Soft Left. I do not say that a Tory Government can do no wrong; but it is surely bizarre (and biased) to claim, every time the Prime Minister opens his mouth, that he *must* be in the wrong. It has come very close to that.

This is the centre of the whole debate about religion and politics. The Settlement removed the Church from party – i.e. partisan politics. It is not the Church's job to run the country. It is not the Church's job to be political, in the sense that it stands for a set of political policies. Rather it should give politicians, and individual citizens, something higher upon which to make and form their political opinions. It should educate and inform our consciences by teaching, preaching and expounding the Bible and Christian tradition. Whatever anyone might suggest, Jesus Christ was no Socialist; a Tory neither. Those sorts of political party did not exist in first-century Palestine. All Christ's sayings were said in the context of authoritarian monarchies or international dynasties such as the Roman Empire. We are meant to keep the Commandments, love our neighbour as ourselves and forgive our enemies whether we live under Caligula or the sweetness and light much believed to emanate from Socialist and Green parties.

The Gospel does not tell you which way to vote. It absolutely demands individual religious response and the exercise of charity – 'to live in love and peace with all men'. Of course, a Christian Society should be a decent organisation, but that society and organisation is a result of the implementation of acts of individual human wills. Societies do not make moral judgements: individuals do. And what sort of society we have depends upon the quality of those individual judgements. Society at large cannot be asked to respond to moral injunctions. Obedience and disobedience are functions of the individual free will.

It does not matter that the Archbishop of York lives in a palace, travels first class on the train to the London Synod and generally has most of his expenses paid by the man in the pew through his weekly offering. This may, of course, obstruct him in his desire to sound like a good Socialist. But to be a good Christian he does not need to curse himself for his privilege, only to be charitable with his wealth – which I am sure he is.

Envy is never uglier than when it dresses itself in the clothes of egalitarian politics.

It is sometimes argued that the Anglican Settlement is out of date because it was construed at a time when there were no ethnic and religious minorities in England. This is a very shallow view of the matter. When the Settlement was being hammered out in the sixteenth

and seventeenth centuries, there was more animosity
between Catholic and Protestant than ever there has
been this last generation between Christians and Shi'ite
Muslims. Just recall the events: a King of England
beheaded his wife because of a foreign Pope; a Puritan
militarist killed another King and set the whole nation
at odds in a civil war; archbishops were burnt at the
stake. The degree of ancient bitterness must not be
underestimated.

The Anglican Settlement dealt with the problem of
religious differences by the principle of toleration. Catholics were welcomed at Anglican altars if they came
'soberly and peaceably inclined'. It was the old doctrine
of our duty to the stranger within our gate. It was a truly
one-nation practical philosophy.

The new fashion for 'pluralism' in which there is no
agreed norm or authority – where a Shi'ite in Bradford
is, at his mosque, as much entitled to define himself in
terms of Englishness as the bishop in his cathedral – is
the route to disaster. The Civil War showed us the
unpalatable social truth: Someone must win and then
he must distinguish himself by his magnanimity. (The
fact that this was where Cromwell's men spectacularly
failed goes a long way to accounting for the Restoration
of the Monarchy.)

Pluralism works only where religion is weak.
Weaken religion, then, and abolish strife? But where
religion is weakened and marginalised, in a fit of self-
abnegation as in English Christianity today, what does
the nation live by? It will not live by the bland out-
pourings of utilitarianism. It will be taken over by either
crass materialism (as in the USA) or some violent caricature religion such as exists in Iran. Look at what
happened to the Shah.

Pluralism is never suggested by people who feel strongly about religion, by people who are actually religious, but by others – academics, bishops and the like who derive their security not from the truths of religion, but from the liberal, utilitarian consensus which stands back, as it were, regarding itself as the one point from which all religions can be observed and evaluated. There is no such point in fact.

In the ultimate sense, it is very difficult – perhaps even impossible – to talk about absolute truth in the area of religion. But we do not work in the context of the ultimate, only in that of the political reality – the nation, the realm. Here, it could never do to say, 'Anything might be true.' That is the voice of the progressive Religious Education teacher telling Sharon in 4b to 'make up her own mind' on eternal religious issues. It is the recipe for a breach of the peace, for wars of religion to break out.

The Anglican Settlement was a middle way between dictatorship and anarchy. It is not politically creative or of any practical benefit to say, 'You *must* believe this.' And it is just as bad to say, 'Believe what you like.' The subtle, English, historically workable compromise has been to say, 'This is true and it is what this realm believes. If you are a member of this realm, you will not be required to believe it. We will tolerate your dissent. You are welcome at our altars. Keep the peace.'

Now, in the true sense of the word 'liberal', what could be more generous than that? Certainly not either of the two alternatives most commonly cited, which, as I have said, constitute either tyranny or anarchy.

The reason why *something* must be proclaimed as National Orthodoxy is that the realm is founded upon institutions: it may be Monarchy and Church; it must

certainly involve education, law and policing. It is
bound to determine the form of leisure activities: do we
tolerate alcohol and other drugs (if so, which)? What
degree of undress? of aggression? If everyone can think
and believe just as they like, and all thoughts are equal,
then *practically* chaos is guaranteed. Should Rasta-
farians be made to cease smoking cannabis? Should
motorcycling Sikhs be forced to wear crash helmets?
Even secular liberalism demands that at least, if you
want to go nude, you do so on a nudist beach or in some
other designated area.

The reason why pluralism will not work politically,
socially, is that religion is about the things that are most
basic – and also most practical – in the lives of human
beings. And the different religions disagree on these
basics, sometimes fundamentally. To put all religions
on the same level, therefore, is to say that – *as a matter of
practical conduct* – anything goes so long as you religiously believe it. No realm could peacefully exist on
such a maxim for five minutes. And there is no need to
drag in extreme ethical cases in order to justify this
argument. Never mind the fanatic who religiously believes in human sacrifice: consider only cases such as
are covered by the Obscene Publications Act.

A mature society, one might say a 'settled' society, is
not opinionless. It is confident in its beliefs and tolerant
of dissent. But that means that at least 'Orthodoxy' and
'Dissent' are properly defined. A mature society, a civ-
ilised society, is also proud of its institutions and guards
them. It knows that absolute *laissez-faire* in the matter of
what people may *believe* will sooner or later result in
absolute *laissez-faire* in what people may *do*. It means
that the concept of an institution – as something that
embodies particular values – must vanish. And, plainly,

a society cannot exist without its institutions. Tolerant Orthodoxy is the core of the Anglican Settlement.

Oddly enough, while in the matter of comparative religion, interfaith dialogue and related affairs, the doors have been thrown ever wider – 'Let him believe what he chooses' – within Christianity itself there has been a narrowing. This narrowing is called the Ecumenical Movement. There is something odd about a man who says that, from one religion to another, anything, any diversity, goes; but that, within denominations of a religion, everyone should strive to be – or at least to appear – the same. But this is exactly what is being done in the interdenominational bureaucracy to standardise texts (ARCIC) – to make the Catholic Mass, the Holy Communion and the Methodist Supper of the Lord into literally the same thing. It is positively weird to discover that the man – usually a bishop or an academic – who is most disposed to absolute variation in 'inter-religious dialogue' (as they call it) turns out to be very strict on uniformity when it comes to what Christians of various persuasions should say in their prayers.

Where stands 'Liberalism' now?

Religious denominations sharing a common Creed develop to answer a particular need. So, in the eighteenth century, Methodism began – first as a party within the Church of England and later separate from it – because the excessively latitudinarian (and in some cases bone idle) clergy were neglecting the Gospel. A new form of chapel service evolved based on the words and music of the Wesleys and on extempore prayer. Over two centuries this aspect of English Christianity's tradition has enriched the realm. Until comparatively recently, if I went into the Chapel I expected something different from what happens in Church. There are still differences, of course, but the similarities based on shared texts – more often than not the international jargon foisted on us by the Western Church's equivalent of Brussels bureaucrats – are becoming more noticeable.

So the essential character of Methodism is fast disappearing. As for the Roman Mass, it is almost indistinguishable from Rite 'A' in the *Alternative Service Book*. I cannot believe that unity based on inferior texts is preferable to a diversity which reveals itself in richness of custom and language. In fact, the appearance of unity is an illusion because there are matters of principle which separate Rome from the Church of England – as the Pope reminded the Archbishop of Canterbury in an unambiguous letter as recently as 1989.

It makes no sense to strive for unison in liturgical expression and exact similarity in forms of church services when there are profound differences in moral doctrines and in what is fundamentally believed about matters of life and death.

How, for instance, can Anglicans pray the same prayers as Roman Catholics when one Church affirms the moral benefits of selective abortion and embryo research while the other Church completely denounces both these practices?

These are not peripheral issues; they are basic. And it is nonsense to speak of liturgical and doctrinal agreement while there is disagreement on ethical fundamentals. What would it mean, except that the Churches were saying one thing and doing another?

For all the night thoughts of ARCIC, the mutual backslapping, the Pope and the Archbishop kneeling together at the altar rail in Westminster Abbey, Rome does not accept that Anglican priests' orders are valid. When the Pope last visited English racecourses and the Archbishop of Canterbury, many people hoped for an announcement that the Papal Bull *Apostolicae Curae* (1896) would be repealed. This Bull says that Anglican orders are 'absolutely null and utterly void'. Despite earnest requests from Anglican leaders, and a lot more diplomacy behind closed doors, no repeal came. There are other areas of contention – principles honestly held – which preclude any substantial union of the two Churches: there is the issue of women priests and bishops and the question of whether priests should be allowed to marry.

Why should organic unity be thought desirable in any case? It is usually answered by Ecumenists in the doctrine that division is a scandal – 'our unhappy divisions' – and that unity would improve the missionary work of the whole Church. But are the divisions really scandalous and unhappy? I do not believe so. Denominations, as we have noticed, arise to fulfil a need and this is a psychological, temperamental need as much as anything else. Within a broad band of common consent, people must be allowed breathing space. Some of our theologians think there is nothing wrong when a devout Christian lives in the same town as a devout Muslim but that Christian denominations should strive to abolish their doctrinal differences.

But in reality, there are people who are temperamentally (as well as intellectually) suited by Lutheran Christianity, say, but for whom Catholicism would be entirely unpalatable. Moreover, the abolition of doctrinal differences and the disappearance of denominational characteristics would weaken the

Church's missionary enterprise: precisely because it would remove the opportunity for emotional and temperamental preferences – choice.

The argument that the Church should be 'one' because Christ prayed for unity is spurious and anachronistic. Christ did not envisage a Church in the way it has developed over the centuries: a Church with hierarchies and bureaucracies and Synods, or even a Church with Parochial Church Councils and the Boys' Brigade. It is far more likely that, when he prayed for unity, he was praying that his handful of followers should not fall out among themselves; and that, years later, St John, in his gospel, used Christ's prayer in order to persuade the fledgling Church not to disperse into myriad shades of gnosticism. Such sectarianism was rife in the Middle East in Roman times.

A National Church, then, would not decree that we must all be exactly the same. There have always been differences in custom, posture and emphasis – High, Low and Broad, said or sung, vestments or no vestments. This is an acceptable form of unity in diversity because it provides for various sorts of spiritual, psychological needs while it also retains enough common doctrine for the Church to be described as one and the same thing.

The overwhelming argument for a National Church is that we all inhabit the same plot. Our institutions are natural and national. They are what bind us to this realm which is the predominant political reality. It is rooted in a common language – which was mostly created by the National Church in the first place by the *Authorised Version* and the *Book of Common Prayer* – a shared history and a national culture. It has stood us well for some hundreds of years because it was soundly wrought. Why try to get rid of it, then? 'Why,' as W. H. Auden said, 'spit on our luck?'

And so, to ask for a National Church is not a sentimental act; it is not 'to summon the spectre of a rose, or follow an antique drum'. It is to want to preserve that thing which has given us the real liberties which we have as a nation. It is to want to preserve a way of life, a life of a certain character that has been won out of extreme difficulties. It is the desire to save that which we know does us good against both hidebound and doctrinaire views of the State and fanciful radical abstractions.

Why spit on our luck? It is the desire to be moderate and tolerant, truly liberal and practical – to conserve that which works in daily life.

It is the desire and the need to remain English.